THE ECHO SOUNDER AND FISHFINDER HANDBOOK

THE ECHO SOUNDER AND FISHFINDER HANDBOOK

David Redhouse

fernhurst BOOKS

First published in 1994 by
Fernhurst Books, 33 Grand Parade, Brighton,
East Sussex BN2 2QA

Printed and bound in Great Britain

British Library Cataloguing in Publication Data
A catalogue record for this book is available from the British Library.

ISBN 0-906754-97-6

Acknowledgements

The author and publishers would like to thank the following organisations and individuals
for their help in the preparation of this book:
Lowrance Electronics Inc., John Scott, Simpson-Lawrence Ltd, James Douglas and
Hugh Davies (of Simpson-Lawrence), Mike Phillips of Incastec Associates Ltd, S. M.
International, NASA (1992) Ltd, Adrian Shine of the Loch Ness Project, N. J. Kingston,
R. Williams of Aquascan Ltd, the Fisheries Department of the UK National Rivers
Authority (South West), Sue and Jeri Drake, Steve Mills and Andy Little.

Photographic credits

The photographs and other illustrations reproduced in this book were supplied by the
following individuals and agencies:
Ampro Distribution Ltd: page 60.
Fuso Industries Inc: page 28 (TR).
The Hydrographic Office of the Ministry of Defence: page 78.
Andy Little: page 57.
The Loch Ness and Morar Project: page 90.
Lowrance/Eagle Inc: pages 10 (B), 11, 12 (B), 13 (L), 14 (B), 29, 32 (R), 37, 43, 45, 46,
47, 52, 53, 61, 71 (T), 75, 83 (B), 84, 91 (T), 91 (B), cover.
NASA (1992) Ltd: page 12 (T).
Steve Mills: page 86.
Motor Boat and Yachting magazine: page 85.
David Redhouse: pages 8, 24, 31 (T), 36, 39 (T), 40, 48, 54, 88.
The Sea Fish Industry Authority: page 77.
Underwater World Publications Ltd: page 76.
John Woodward: pages 6, 9, 10 (T), 13 (R), 14 (T), 15 (B), 17, 18, 23, 28 (TL), 28 (B),
30, 31 (B), 32 (L), 39 (B), 41, 44, 64, 66, 67, 69, 71 (B), 72, 79, 82, 83 (T).

The portion of Admiralty chart 1652 on page 81 is Crown Copyright, reproduced from
the chart with the permission of the Controller of Her Majesty's Stationery Office.

DTP by John Woodward
Artwork by Jenny Searle
Cover design by Simon Balley
Printed and bound by Ebenezer Baylis & Son, Worcester

CONTENTS

INTRODUCTION ·····························

The echo sounder has come a long way from the days when it simply showed the depth of water under your keel. Modern sounders can display a wealth of information about the nature of the sea bed, the objects lying on it and the fish swimming above it. Many units are also combined with GPS electronic navigators, enabling users to plot their discoveries and return to the same sites again and again. For sports users such as anglers and divers, commercial operators such as inshore fishermen, construction companies and those engaged in marine scientific research the echo sounder is an invaluable tool – not only for indicating the depth, showing fish underwater and locating objects such as wrecks and obstructions on the sea bed, but also for building up bottom profiles to pinpoint reefs, ledges and gullies. In short, it is an underwater window.

There are several different types of sounder available – including video units, liquid crystal displays and paper recorders. If you are thinking of buying an echo sounder, or a combined sounder and GPS navigator, you are probably con-

cerned that you may spend a lot of money only to end up with the wrong model for your needs. If you already own a machine, you may feel you could get a lot more from your investment.

Either way, this book will help you. Using straightforward terminology, it explains how to choose a sounder or combined sounder/navigator, and how to use it more effectively by both explaining the functions of the controls and, perhaps more importantly, how to interpret the pictures on the screen. Absolutely no technical knowledge is required, and any terminology is fully explained. If you've given up with the handbook, read on!

Since many of these machines are manufactured in the USA it is worth noting that they are often described as sonar units in American sales brochures. In the UK the word sonar stands for SOund NAvigation and Ranging, and describes a piece of similar but more complex equipment that scans through 360 degrees rather like an underwater radar. This is used by commercial fishermen, and by the navy to hunt for submarines, and is outside the scope of this book.

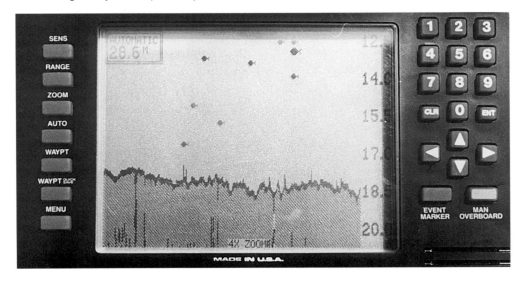

1 CHOOSING A SOUNDER ·······················

Before considering the choice of equipment currently available, let's have a brief look at the development of the echo sounder.

The lead line

Until the end of the last century, all soundings were taken using a lead line. This was a length of cord some 25 fathoms long with a hollowed lead weight attached to its end. The cord had coloured markers made of different materials tied on at measured intervals as follows:

At 2 fathoms — Leather with two ends.
At 3 fathoms — Leather with three ends.
At 5 fathoms — White calico.
At 7 fathoms — Red bunting.
At 10 fathoms — Leather with a hole in it.
At 13 fathoms — Blue serge.
At 15 fathoms — White calico.
At 17 fathoms — Red bunting.
At 20 fathoms — Strand of cord with two
                        knots in it.

The depth of water could be read by observing the coloured marker nearest the surface, or at night by feeling the material. This information was called to the helmsman as 'by the mark' and the number of fathoms or, for the intervening depths known as deeps, 'by the deep'. Halves and quarters of a fathom would be calculated and called by the leadsman – who would always subtract a quarter for safety.

A lump of tallow could be placed in the hollow in the lead to bring up a specimen of the bottom. This was called 'arming the lead' and could be a useful navigation aid in bad visibility. The sea bed material is still marked on charts for this purpose.

Some skill was required to swing the lead, which was always cast on the windward side of sailing craft so that the leeway of the vessel would not cause it to foul the stern gear. It had to be swung forward when the vessel was moving, so that the line was vertical and therefore giving an accurate reading by the time the ship had drawn level. This system of depth finding was normal for small craft until quite recently, and it still has its uses.

Mechanical sounding

In the 1870s Lord Kelvin began a series of experiments with a device that reacted to changes in water pressure, to see if it could be used to measure depth. His experimental device was developed into the Kelvin Mark 4 sounding machine, which was used by the Royal Navy until the outbreak of the Second World War.

The machine was basically a glass tube, open at one end and coated inside with chromate of silver. Normally red-brown, the chemical turned white upon exposure to salt water. The deeper the tube was lowered, the more the air inside it was compressed by the rising water

LEFT **Swinging the lead, circa 1800. The sailor stands in the chains, one of a number of small platforms on the outside of the hull.**

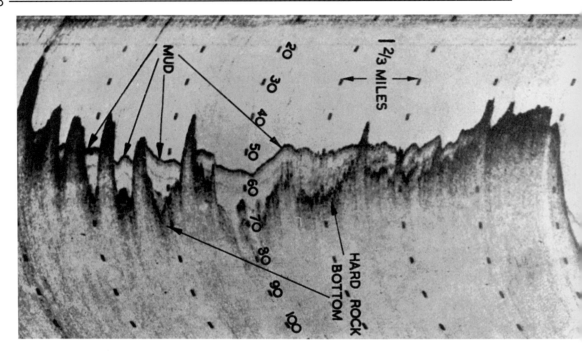

MUD

20
30
40
50
60
70
80
90
100

← 1²/₃ MILES →

HARD ROCK
BOTTOM

pressure. This allowed the water level within the tube to rise – and be recorded by the reaction of the silver chromate.

The tube was placed inside a brass sinker, drilled with a number of holes to allow the water in. The whole assembly was lowered to the sea bed on the end of a length of wire. When the wire went slack, indicating that the sinker had touched bottom, it was wound up again. On recovery, the point where the silver chromate changed colour was measured against a pre-determined scale to find the depth of water.

Hydrophones

Around 1909, some American engineers started generating and receiving very low-frequency ultrasonic pulses in water using a device which was developed into the hydrophone.

The Admiralty 752 hydrophone of the 1930s was based around a transmitter that produced sound impulses at the rate of three per second, generated by an electrically-driven spring hammer striking a steel diaphragm in a tank on the ship's

ABOVE **A remarkably good trace from an Admiralty 753 recorder, obtained during trials in 1937. Note the way the recording shows a layer of mud overlying rock on the sea bed – a result that is possible only on machines which use very low audio frequencies. A modern sports fishing sounder would simply show the top of the mud as the bottom.**

hull. These audible signals travelled from the ship's hull to the sea bed and back again, to be received by a similar device on another part of the hull. This converted the signals back into electrical pulses that could be heard on headphones, and by constantly tuning the set to receive the clearest signal, and checking the tuning against a pre-determined scale, the operator could monitor the depth.

Manuals of the period suggest that operator ear fatigue was a problem, and in 1937 the receiver was replaced by the 753 model paper recorder in which a rotating stylus marked a roll of paper by liberating iodine within the paper to produce a sepia stain. Surprisingly good pictures of the sea bed were obtained by these audio-frequency machines.

ABOVE **A Seafarer Seascribe Mk 1 of 1970-76, both closed (left) and open to show the rotating arm that held both the stylus and a flashing neon. Note the curious curvilinear trace.**

Ultrasonic types

In a parallel development in the early 1930s the Kelvin Hughes Company, co-founded by Lord Kelvin, developed an ultrasonic recording sounder based on a transducer operating on the magneto striction principle, in which a stack of thin nickel plates vibrated when exposed to a magnetic field to produce a pulse of energy.

The first Kelvin Hughes paper recording echo sounder, the MS1, came on the market in 1933, and users soon noticed that their machines were recording signals in mid-water, well above the sea bed – fish! In 1935 a Norwegian fishing research vessel used an MS3 to positively identify cod and herring shoals – and so the fishfinder was born. (The prefix M.S., used on all the Kelvin Hughes echo sounders, derives from the initial letters of the words magneto striction.)

Paper recording sounders

These machines worked well, but because of their size and cost they were effectively restricted to commercial operators. The development of micro-electronics in the sixties and early seventies changed all this, since it enabled companies such as Ferrograph and Seafarer in the UK, Lowrance in the USA and others in Japan to develop reasonably lightweight machines at prices that sports users could afford.

By this time the wet iodine-impregnated paper used in paper recorders had been superseded by a dry electro-sensitive type, onto which the picture was electrically etched as it slowly moved under a rotating pen or stylus. Models such as the Seafarer Seascribe marked the paper with a stylus mounted on a rotor assembly, giving a rather strange curvilinear representation of the sea bed and fish. On most machines the marked paper was fed out of the case through a slot in the side or base so that it could be easily cut and removed for scrutiny – although on small boats it could become a rather soggy mess in bad weather!

These machines were often of the flasher/graph type in which the rotating arm held both a stylus for marking the paper and a flashing neon light to indicate depth in non-recording mode.

The rotating-arm machines were soon superseded by relatively low-cost straight-line devices in which the stylus moved vertically down the paper on a rubber belt. This gave an undistorted image similar to the pictures produced by today's liquid crystal machines. In the early eighties machines of this type produced by Japanese manufacturers such as Fuji Royal – who produced the popular R.F. 600 and R.F. 700 models followed by the R.F.210 series – and Honda, whose products were sold in Europe by Kelvin Hughes under their own and the Depmar

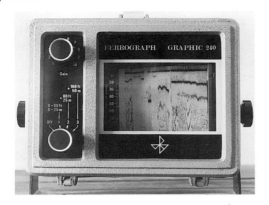

ABOVE **A Ferrograph Graphic 240 of the 1970s, showing the undistorted image created by the straight-line movement of the stylus.**

brand names, dominated what was then a relatively small sports fishing and diving market.

In late 1983, the Lowrance Company of the USA launched the Eagle Mach 1, a development of their computerised X15 machine introduced a year earlier. The picture quality and range versatility of this sounder ensured that it immediately became the best-selling paper sounder worldwide – a position it maintained until being discontinued in 1993. The later X16 model with multi-function keyboard is still widely used by serious anglers and fishermen.

BELOW **The Eagle Mach 1 – a modern paper sounder that became a worldwide best-seller.**

Over the last few years sales of paper sounders have dropped dramatically with the growing sophistication of the liquid crystal models. Compared with these, paper recorders are bulky and awkward, and they are not totally waterproof. The constant stream of fine carbon dust caused by the stylus etching the paper makes regular cleaning essential, otherwise the dust clogs the paper driving gears, and both the stylus and stylus belt wear out and need replacing from time to time. Paper recorders do not have the alarm, digital, fish ID, or other computerised functions of liquid crystal models, and finally there is always the expense of the paper.

But this does not mean that they are obsolete. Although relatively few machines are now available – notably from the Lowrance company – they are still valued because their high picture quality or resolution enables underwater objects to be observed in more detail than is possible on video or liquid crystal models. They are also the only machines that produce a permanent record for comparison and future reference.

Flashing and digital sounders

Although they are now rarely used by sea anglers and divers because of their lack of sophistication, it is worth having a look at flashing sounders.

Developed in the late fifties and early sixties, again by companies like Lowrance in the USA and Seafarer in the UK, flash-

ABOVE **A flashing sounder – simple but effective, and still preferred by many yachtsmen.**

ing sounders displayed the depth as a spot of light on a circular dial some four to five inches across. The spot of light was generated by a neon or a light-emitting diode (LED) which flashed when the transducer pulse was transmitted and received. The light source was positioned at the end of a rotating arm, so a longer time interval between transmission and reception of the pulse – and hence deeper water – allowed the arm to rotate further around the dial before flashing. Owing to the speed of the rotor the flashes merged to give the effect of a continuous light indicating the depth.

Interestingly, many manufacturers designed their sets with 'clock face' dials showing a shallow-water scale of 0-60 feet. This was useful because the transmit flash always appeared at the 12 o'clock position, enabling the receive flash – showing the depth – to be judged by relating it to the minute hand on an imaginary clock face. So '20 minutes past', for example, indicated a depth of 20 feet. This made the display easy to read at night, and made backlighting unnecessary.

In the UK these machines were designed for use as depth finders for yachts, but in the USA many manufacturers looked to sports fishermen for their market since it was found that fish would show up as secondary flashes on the dial. Information about the kind of bottom

under the boat could also be discerned by the experienced user.

A more recent development has been the digital sounder, which uses microprocessor technology to display depths as figures on a liquid crystal display. Since no interpretation of the signal is possible this type of sounder can only be used for navigation.

Video sounders

A video sounder displays the picture on a cathode ray tube just like a domestic TV. Both colour and monochrome versions are available. On the more popular colour models the different colours are used to represent different strengths of echo. The strongest signals – such as the sea bed – are normally indicated by red, while the weaker signals are displayed progressively as orange, yellow, green, and two or three shades of blue.

Colour video sounders are favoured by commercial fishermen because the large display can be easily seen from across a wheelhouse and the different colours make for quick and easy interpretation of the signals. These sets have good resolution, since the picture is composed of many small dots, as in a television set. The colour presentation makes for easy interpretation and many zoom, digital and alarm functions are available. Another advantage is that most models will run on a 24-volt dc supply as well as a 12-volt supply, whereas liquid crystal models are normally restricted to 12 volts only.

The main disadvantage of video sounders is that they are not fully waterproof, and the high voltages used in the display make them unsuitable for 'wet' locations. This, combined with the fact that the picture will fade in sunlight, means that they must be installed in sheltered, shady positions, and this makes them unsuitable for open boats. They are also rather bulky, and they consume a significant amount of power: normally between 1-2 amps. Furthermore, incorrect adjustment of the sensitivity control can produce anomalous colouring which gives

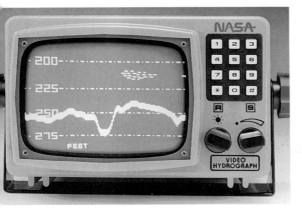

ABOVE **The Nasa Video hydrograph, a budget-priced sounder with a TV-type display.**

very small echoes the appearance of large targets.

Owing to the popularity of liquid crystal sets few low-cost video models are available. One exception is the monochrome Video Hydrograph produced by the British Nasa company which, at the time of writing, sells for roughly the price of a modest TV set in the UK. The cheapest colour units cost roughly three times as much.

BELOW **A Lowrance X55 liquid crystal sounder – lightweight, compact, waterproof and practical.**

Liquid crystal sounders

Finally we come to the liquid crystal graph (LCG) echo sounder which currently dominates the sport fishing and diving markets.

LCG sounders are lightweight, compact and fully sealed against the elements – indeed the Lowrance and Eagle models are pressurised with an inert gas, making them totally waterproof, and the screens are condensation-free so they can be mounted in exposed outside positions, making them ideal for use on rigid-hull inflatables (RIBs) and other 'wet' boats.

An LCG screen displays a black or blue-grey picture on an almost colourless background, and all recent models have a supertwist display making them easier to read at an angle. They are also easy to read in bright sunlight, again making them ideal for small-boat use. The contrast on the latest models has been improved still further by displaying the information on a very light green background.

A few years ago the Hummingbird company introduced a model that displayed fish as red dots, followed by a model with a full-colour LCD display. Unfortunately both had to be discontinued owing to high production costs, and currently there are no colour LCG sounders on the market.

This is hardly a problem, however, since even low-priced models are crammed with features. These include a digital readout of depth, fish and depth alarms, multiple zoom ranges and fish identification modes. They take relatively little juice from your battery – some models using only 0.25 amps – and because of this you can now buy totally portable versions which run on two lantern batteries housed in a box slung under the display.

Some disadvantages include the fact that the displays are rather small compared with their video and paper counterparts, and some of the earlier models gave a rather blocky screen presentation. Nevertheless, a great deal of underwater information can be obtained from an LCG fishfinder – as thousands of sports users can testify.

2 EQUIPMENT INSTALLATION ·····················

It is often said that buying a piece of boat equipment is the easy bit. Your problems start when you attempt to install it – particularly if you have to drill holes below the waterline…

Fortunately the modern liquid crystal echo sounder is designed with owner installation in mind, and fitting the unit to a fibreglass angling boat or RIB will normally take little more than an hour of the owner's time. Colour video and paper sounders require a little more planning because of their power requirements and bulk, and installations in wooden and steel hulled craft can also involve a few complications.

That said, installing a modern fishfinder is a relatively simple task. Detailed instructions are supplied by all the well-known manufacturers and most of the specialist retailers can offer information and advice if you encounter any particular problems.

BELOW **A liquid crystal display unit and mounting bracket, power lead and transducer ready for installation.**

FITTING THE DISPLAY

All sounders are supplied with a bracket for table-top mounting, and the best place is usually near the steering position or on the shelf behind the windscreen. A flush mounting facility is available from some manufacturers; this allows the instrument to be recessed into an instrument panel or console. Some sets can be overhead-mounted, but not all, so check if this is your intention. A colour video sounder will have to be positioned in a relatively sheltered and shady part of the boat since these sounders are not waterproof, and their screens fade in direct sunlight.

Liquid crystal sounders have very little metal in their construction and can usually be positioned within an inch or two of a compass without affecting it, but a paper recorder or video sounder must be further away – perhaps one or two feet, depending on the model.

BELOW **Mounting the set ahead of the steering position is ideal.The steering compass on this RIB was quite unaffected by the sounder display.**

ABOVE **The rear of an LCG showing the connections for transducer and power leads.**

One of the advantages of buying a liquid crystal echo sounder is its very low power consumption of between 0.25 amp and 0.75 amp. This means that, even if you do not have charging facilities on your boat, you will still get a good weekend's use from, say, a 20 amp motorcycle battery – and even longer from a 60-80 amp car battery. All sounders are supplied with a power lead that plugs into the back of the set, and this can be run either to a switch panel or directly to the battery, red lead to positive and black to negative. (Note however that some Japanese sounders have a white positive lead.) Most sounders are polarity protected, so they will not be damaged if the power leads are reversed; they simply won't switch on.

An in-line fuse is normally supplied by the manufacturer to give protection from power surges, but it is a relatively crude device. Do not be tempted to connect the set direct to the charging system of an outboard, since spikes of high voltage will soon leave your investment worthless.

Remember that paper recording and colour sounders require more power than LCGs; two amps or more in some cases.

Many users remove the sounder display unit from the boat at the end of the day for security reasons. If you do this make sure the power lead is disconnected from the battery, or the minute electric current always present will corrode the positive pin in the plug through electrolytic action with the atmosphere.

FITTING THE TRANSDUCER

The transducer consists of a ceramic element embedded in a plastic casing. When it receives an electrical signal from the display this element vibrates to transmit a pulse of energy through the water. When the pulse of energy returns from the sea bed, the reverse happens and an electrical signal is sent from the element to the display for processing.

There are several styles of transducer mounting, so check which type you are getting when you buy your sounder. If you need a non-standard fitting your retailer should be able to arrange a swap.

Transom mounting

Most American-made liquid crystal sounders are supplied with a transom-mounted transducers as standard equipment. These transducers are ideal for stern-drive or outboard powered angling boats and RIBs, particularly planing boats and boats with cathedral hulls where the transom is often the only part of the boat in contact with a good solid lump of water.

BELOW **A typical transom-mounted transducer. The bracket is screwed to the boat and the transducer bolted to the bracket.**

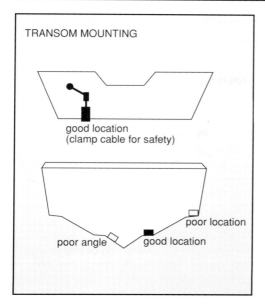

TRANSOM MOUNTING

good location
(clamp cable for safety)

poor angle   good location   poor location

The most recent models are hydrodynamically designed with a rounded, torpedo shaped profile to cause the minimum of water turbulence both around the face of the transducer and behind the boat.

A transom-mounted transducer must be installed below the waterline using bolts or self-tapping screws, with the face pointing straight down. Ideally the base of the transducer should be level with the bottom of the boat. If it is positioned in front of the outboard or stern-drive propeller it will not be affected by propeller turbulence, except of course when the boat is going astern, and a kick-up facility prevents damage by semi-submerged objects. On most American LCGs the transducer is attached to its bracket by a single bolt, so it can be be swivelled up against the transom to protect it when beach launching.

Many manufacturers also offer a variation of this transducer with a suction cup mount. Although really designed for freshwater use, since they tend to pull off at speed, owners of smaller craft may find them useful in inshore waters if a permanent fitting is inconvenient.

Some of the Japanese models only offer a transducer designed for through-hull mounting: a circular head with a four-inch threaded stem. Although this type *can* be transom mounted with a small bracket, it has no kick-up facility and tends to look more awkward on the back of the boat than the streamlined American type.

In-hull mounting

On some boats, such as those with inboard engines where the propellers are forward of the transom, it is not possible to transom-mount the transducer because the disturbed water passing under it would disrupt the signal. Transom-mounted transducers also look out of place on many larger craft. In such cases you may need to consider a different method of installation.

If the boat is constructed of single skin fibreglass (GRP), a transducer can be mounted inside the hull – provided the GRP is not more than, say, 0.75 inches thick. Most American in-hull (also called shoot-thru-hull) transducers come in the form of a small circular pod, which is stuck to the inside of the hull using a two-part epoxy resin supplied by the manufacturer.

Once again, it is important that the transducer is pointing straight down, and that it is located over a part of the hull which has a smooth flow of water moving under it. The quality of hull construction under the transducer must be good, with

BELOW **An in-hull transducer mounted on a bed of epoxy. Remember to clean the GRP and roughen it with sandpaper before applying the epoxy.**

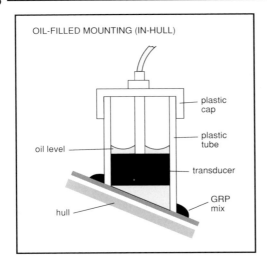

OIL-FILLED MOUNTING (IN-HULL)

- plastic cap
- plastic tube
- oil level
- transducer
- GRP mix
- hull

no air bubbles in the laminate, because the signal will be distorted by the air.

If you are unsure of a good in-hull location, anchor your boat in about 60 feet of water, switch on the display and, with a dab of grease or vaseline on the face of the transducer, push it up against the hull

TRANSDUCER POSITIONS: INBOARD ENGINES

slightly aft of midships on displacement boat

nearer stern on planing boat

transducer must always be mounted forward of propeller or any obstructions on the hull

in various places to find the location that gives the best picture on the screen.

If the hull is of double-skin foam sandwich construction the transducer must be installed on the outer skin, since it is not able to transmit through the air gap between the skins.

If the hull is steeply angled, try mounting the transducer on a small horizontal platform of epoxy or similar material so it points straight down. An alternative is to cut the base of a plastic tube to an angle that matches the deadrise of the hull, and glue it in place. Insert the transducer, then fill the tube below the face of the transducer with a liquid. Any liquid will do the job, but castor oil is often preferred because it has a lower freezing temperature than water, and is not so likely to generate air bubbles in rough weather.

Whichever method is used, it is important that the transducer is facing straight down, and that there is a solid or liquid interface between the transducer and the hull The presence of any air will severely degrade the sounder's performance.

Through-hull mounting

The main advantage of mounting the transducer inside the hull is obvious: it requires no holes beneath the waterline, and the job can be done while the boat is on the water. Some attenuation of the signal is inevitable, however, and the thicker the hull, the worse the problem. So it is not recommended if you aim to go fishfinding in very deep water, or if the boat has a thick hull. In-hull mounting cannot be used on wooden, aluminium or steel hulled boats, and the only option – assuming transom mounting is not possible – is to get out the drill and mount a transducer through the hull.

A through-hull transducer has a four- or five-inch threaded stem which is pushed up from underneath the hull through a hole just wide enough to accept it. The device is held firm by a large nut and washer screwed on from inside the hull. As before, the transducer should be positioned vertically in an area of the hull that

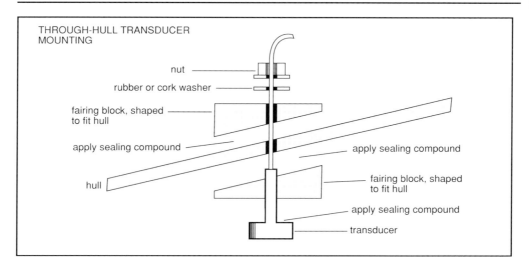

THROUGH-HULL TRANSDUCER
MOUNTING

nut

rubber or cork washer

fairing block, shaped
to fit hull

apply sealing compound

hull

apply sealing compound

fairing block, shaped
to fit hull

apply sealing compound

transducer

is free from turbulence, normally slightly aft of midships.

Bronze transducers are popular with commercial boats (and are required by Lloyds) but they are expensive. Many manufacturers offer a plastic through-hull model which is cheaper, although it has a thicker stem to maintain the same strength. In any case you have to use a plastic transducer on a steel or aluminium boat. This is because different metals in contact with one another in sea water corrode through the effects of electrolysis.

Although some through-hull transducers are streamlined it is best to fit a fairing block around the transducer head, especially on a curved hull. The fairing block will not only protect the transducer head – both from submerged flotsam and in the event of a grounding – but will also help smooth out the water flow and so reduce water interference.

One or two owners of wooden and steel boats have installed in-hull transducers on 'windows' of epoxy or fibreglass resin covering holes drilled right through the hull, but recent improvements in transducer design have made such complictaions unnecessary. One leading manufacturer has introduced a model that protrudes only slightly from the hull and is secured and protected by a saucer-shaped flange. Another model has a flush mount with a chamfered head, allowing it to be embedded in the hull so that there is no projection whatsoever.

Maintenance

Whatever type of transducer you install, you must keep it free of weed. You can lightly anti-foul through-hull and transom-mounted models if the craft is kept permanently in the water, but otherwise – and ideally – simply clean the transducer face with a little soapy water.

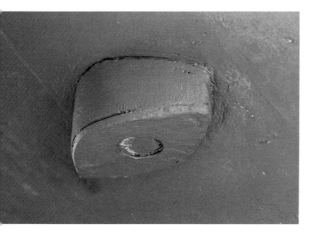

BELOW **The head of a through-hull transducer, streamlined and protected by a fairing block shaped to keep the transducer vertical against the deadrise of the hull.**

You have now chosen, purchased and installed your sounder, and are motoring out to a quiet spot of water to see what it can do.

Most modern liquid crystal models have an automatic control which is activated as soon as the 'on' button is pushed. This locks the sounder onto the sea bed, presenting the bottom signal half to three-quarters of the way down the screen. Any significant variation in depth triggers an automatic range change.

The bottom profile then scrolls across the screen from right to left; but where on that screen are you?

Surprisingly, perhaps, your boat is always at the top right-hand side of the display, and the area of water underneath you is always on the far right of the screen. All the rest of the screen to the left shows the water and sea bed you have already travelled over.

At first, this may seem an odd arrangement. Why, for instance, are you not in the centre of the display? To answer this question, we need to look in detail at what happens from the moment you switch on your sounder.

When you press the 'on' switch an electronic signal is sent from the display to the transducer, which converts that signal into a pulse of high-frequency sound energy. The pulse is transmitted down through the water until it is reflected from the bottom, or by a fish. The returning pulse is received by the transducer and converted

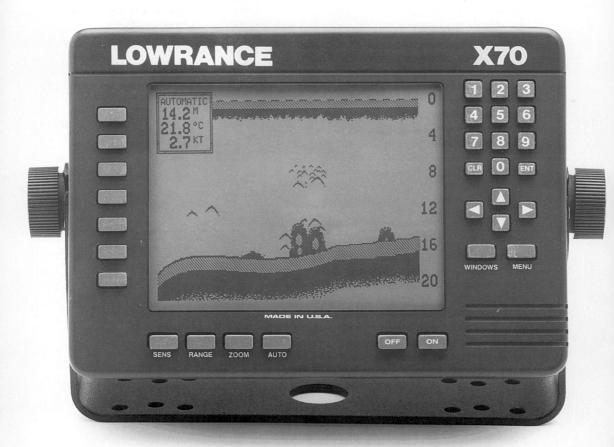

BUILDING UP THE PICTURE

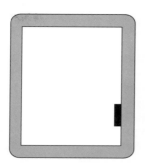  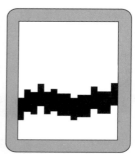

The first pulse echo is displayed on the right-hand side of the screen (shown well over scale and 'blocky' for clarity)

When the second pulse echo is received the first line on the display moves one step to the left and is replaced by a new line of information

Several seconds later the first two lines have scrolled to the far left and the picture has built up across the screen

back to an electronic signal. This is then processed by the machine and presented in the form of marks or pixels corresponding to the relative positions of the bottom and any fish. These marks appear along a vertical line on the far right-hand side of the display. (In the case of a paper sounder, this would be a single stroke of the stylus.)

Immediately, the process is repeated, and the first vertical line of information moves one step to the left to be replaced by a new one. This procedure occurs several times a second and results in the presentation of a continuous scrolling picture of the sea bed, fish and any other underwater features that moves from left to right across the display.

You can adjust the scrolling speed or even stop it if you want to examine a particular part of the picture. It is important to remember that on most sounders the

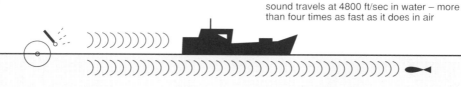

sound travels at 4800 ft/sec in water – more than four times as fast as it does in air

Essentially, the sounder generates an electrical impulse which is converted into a sound wave and transmitted into the water. When this wave strikes an obstacle it rebounds. Since the speed of sound in water is known – and constant – the time lapse between the transmitted signal and the received echo can be measured and the distance to the obstacle determined. The echo sounder can both send and receive sound waves, as well as time, measure and record them.

scrolling speed bears no relation to the speed of the boat, and is adjusted independently. For the best picture quality you should use a fast scrolling speed and slow boat speed of between two and six knots.

On a few sounders with log inputs you can correlate the scrolling and boat speeds so that the area covered by the screen remains the same at different boat speeds.

All sounders display the sea bed as a straight line when the boat is stationary on calm water, because although the screen is still scrolling, it is receiving information from exactly the same place on the sea bed.

Finally, you may notice that in deeper water, when a lower range has been selected, the scrolling speed will automatically slow down. This is to keep the display in step with the longer time delay between the transmission and reception of the sounder pulse.

BOTTOM SIGNAL INTERPRETATION

You have probably noticed that the bottom signal is rarely a pencil-thin line on the screen. In shallow water, indeed, the bottom signal can be an inch or more wide on some models. So why is this?

The answer lies in the way the ultrasonic pulse is transmitted from the transducer. The pulse travels down a roughly cone-shaped path to the bottom, where it paints a roughly circular 'footprint' before being reflected back to the transducer for processing.

Take a look at the diagram. You will see that the centre part of the beam, labelled A, will reach the bottom and return to the transducer microseconds before the outer sides B, C and D. These take longer because they have progressively further to travel. So the edge of the 'footprint' is displayed as deeper than the centre, resulting in the wide line representing the sea bed.

It is a common misconception that the thickness of the bottom signal on the screen represents a certain amount of penetration of the sea bed by the beam of ultrasound. This is not normally the case for the reasons just described, and a few years ago, as part of my glamorous duties as a echo sounder salesman, I had an opportunity of verifying this. I was asked to give a demonstration at a sewage works, to some engineers who were looking for a way of electronically determining the depth of sludge underwater in the sewage holding tanks. Unfortunately for them we were able to prove, using a long pole, that the sounder – an Eagle Mach 1

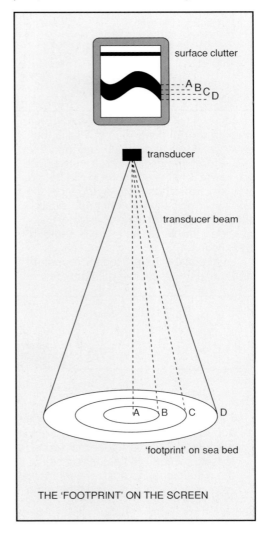

surface clutter

transducer

transducer beam

'footprint' on sea bed

THE 'FOOTPRINT' ON THE SCREEN

– would only display the top of the sludge. The signal indicated no penetration whatsoever, even of this very soft material.

Only specialist survey sounders, which use a combination of very narrow beam angles, high power and low frequencies, are able to give sub-bottom information.

Identifying hard and soft ground

Although no penetration takes place, it is possible to discern the nature of the sea bed by interpretation – so let's look again at the signal reflected from the bottom footprint.

The strength of this signal is not consistent across its width, but strong at the centre and progressively weaker towards the outsides. In shallow water most of the pulse is returned to the transducer to give a wide bottom signal on the display. In deeper water only the stronger centre part of the pulse returns, producing a much narrower line on the screen, as shown in the diagram below. Similarly, a hard rocky sea bed will always reflect more of the weaker pulse than a soft muddy one, to give a wider bottom signal on the screen. You may also see longer tails extending

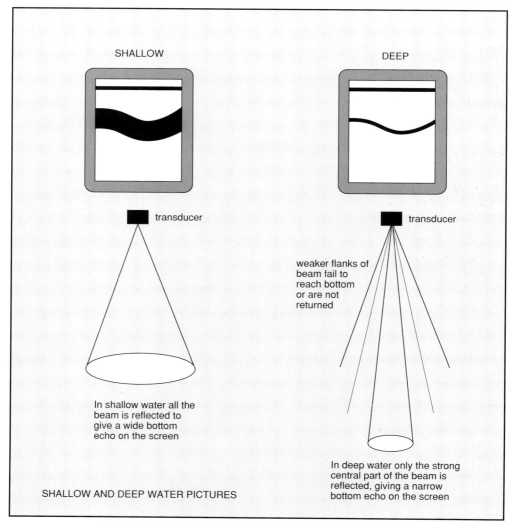

SHALLOW

DEEP

transducer

transducer

weaker flanks of beam fail to reach bottom or are not returned

In shallow water all the beam is reflected to give a wide bottom echo on the screen

In deep water only the strong central part of the beam is reflected, giving a narrow bottom echo on the screen

SHALLOW AND DEEP WATER PICTURES

below the normal bottom signal. This indicates areas of rock or harder ground within a predominantly softer sea bed.

With experience, therefore, you will be able to get a good idea of the nature of the bottom at any given depth from the width of the signal displayed on the screen. Bear in mind, though, that on a sloping sea bed the bottom footprint becomes elongated, and therefore will produce a wider bottom signal on the screen.

If you have used a sounder, you may have seen, particularly in shallow water, a second or even third bottom echo at exactly twice or three times the depth of water. These secondary echoes are caused by the returning bottom signal reflecting off the water surface, going down once again to the sea bed, then returning to give a second trace. Clearly, in all but the shallowest water this would only happen over a hard bottom which produces strong echoes – so this effect

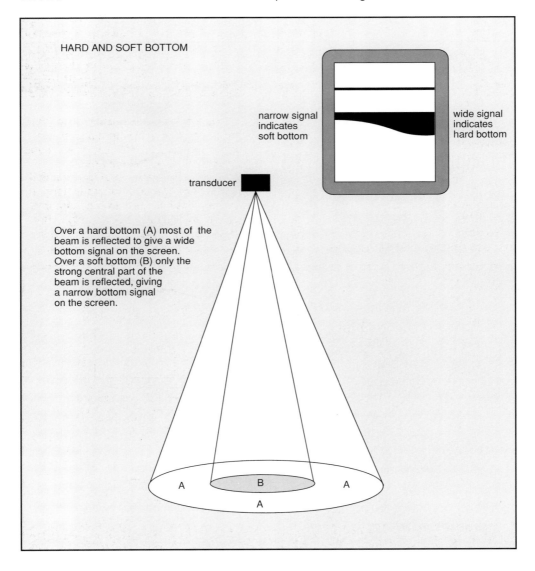

HARD AND SOFT BOTTOM

narrow signal indicates soft bottom

wide signal indicates hard bottom

transducer

Over a hard bottom (A) most of the beam is reflected to give a wide bottom signal on the screen. Over a soft bottom (B) only the strong central part of the beam is reflected, giving a narrow bottom signal on the screen.

A   B   A

A

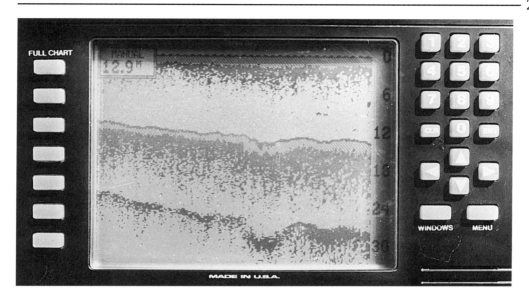

ABOVE **A Lowrance X-70 showing 12.9 metres of water. Although the display shows that the boat is moving into deeper water a widening grey line and a more pronounced secondary echo indicate that the sea bed is harder.**

can be used as an indication of the hardness of the sea bed.

To obtain a secondary echo, set your range to slightly more than double your depth and increase the sensitivity or gain so that the secondary bottom signal *just* shows on the screen. With experience you will be able to judge the softness of the bottom by the appearance of the signal: if it becomes stronger the bottom is becoming harder, and if it starts to break up and disappear, the bottom is becoming softer. The sounder will obviously have to be in manual mode to allow this adjustment.

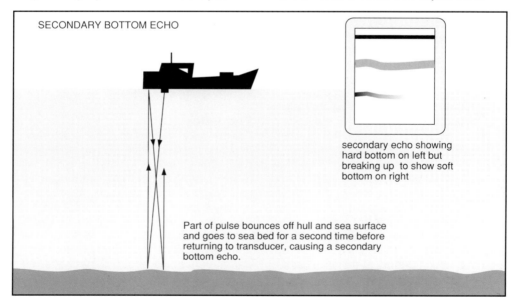

SECONDARY BOTTOM ECHO

secondary echo showing hard bottom on left but breaking up to show soft bottom on right

Part of pulse bounces off hull and sea surface and goes to sea bed for a second time before returning to transducer, causing a secondary bottom echo.

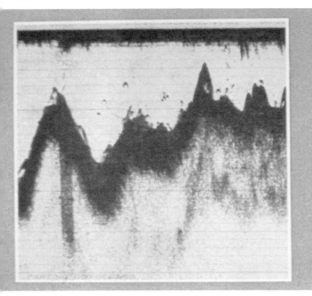 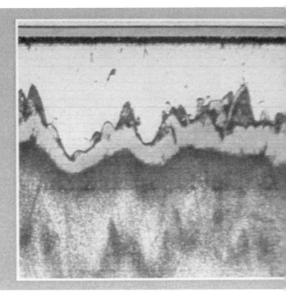

Greyline

This is one of the most misunderstood, yet useful functions of a modern recording echo sounder.

Also known as white line, it was developed in the fifties by the British company Kelvin Hughes, to enable commercial fishermen to locate bottom-feeding fish. The display simply processes the incoming echoes to mark them in black for a short time before changing the colour to white or grey. Strong echo returns from the bottom, for example, will revert to black, to produce the characteristic white or grey band. This means that fish on the bottom do not merge into an otherwise totally black bottom signal, but can be identified as a thickening of the line over the white or grey area.

This function has had many spin-offs. Since the sounder only starts to mark the white or grey band on echoes over a certain signal strength, the size of the fish or fish shoals can, with experience, be more easily judged if the relevant signal on the display begins to grey line. It also follows that a hard bottom produces a wider grey area than a soft bottom at a similar depth – again because of the greater signal strength of the returning echo.

ABOVE **A pair of paper graphs showing the effect of the grey line facility over a rocky sea bed with boulders. With the grey line off (left) everything merges into a thick black bottom signal, but with the grey line on (right) the boulders appear to 'sit' on the grey line much as they sit on the sea bed.**

Furthermore, wrecks and other objects that are not an integral part of the sea bed can be clearly identified on the bottom since they appear to 'sit' on top of the grey line.

Once again the grey or white line is not showing any penetration of the bottom — it is simply a method of processing the incoming signal.

Side lobes

For the sake of simplicity, manufacturers describe the transducer as transmitting a cone-shaped beam. In fact this is not really the case since the transmitted pulse is more cigar-shaped, with a number of secondary beams called side lobes. This is called the *polar pattern*, and the beam width described in the manufacturer's literature is calculated from certain strength parameters at the edges of that pattern.

It helps to know this, since it explains why you sometimes see ghost echoes on

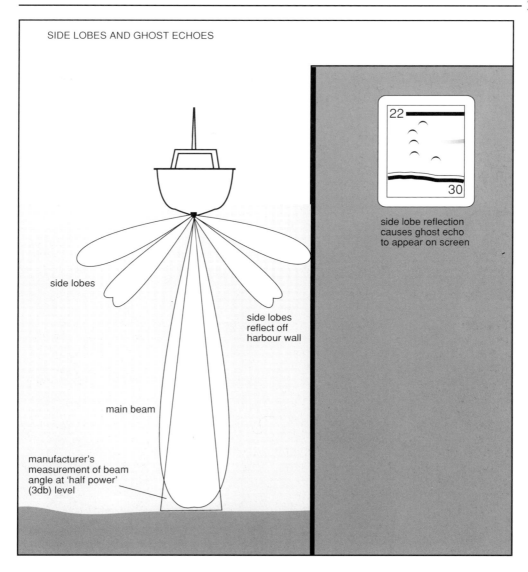

SIDE LOBES AND GHOST ECHOES

22

30

side lobe reflection
causes ghost echo
to appear on screen

side lobes

side lobes
reflect off
harbour wall

main beam

manufacturer's
measurement of beam
angle at 'half power'
(3db) level

the sounder display when the boat is near a harbour wall, or moving in shallow water over a steeply shelving bank. In such areas you may see a ghosting above the bottom that can be mistaken for a bottom feature such as a wreck. The ghosting is caused by the side lobe echo returning to the transducer fractionally before the main pulse, to be indicated on the display as a shallower feature than the bottom mark.

4 OPERATION AND CONTROLS ················

A few years ago a sounder was launched market that had just one knob – to switch it on and off. It was a portable, single-range paper sounder made by Fuji Royal. Although not a best-seller in its time, I think that many users, faced with the complex control panels of today's machines, might prefer a unit with just one knob.

But the complex controls of a modern sounder are a reflection of its versatility. To get the best out of your investment it is worth taking time to become familiar with its functions: how to call them up and how to adjust them.

Range

So what do we mean by range? It is simply the length of the column of water under the boat displayed on the screen, plus a little bit more so the bottom signal shows on the display. In the diagram below the sea bed is at 55 feet, so we have selected a range of 60 feet on the sounder. This is a convenient range because it shows all the water under the boat, plus the bottom signal, and none of the screen area is wasted.

Note the digital read-outs: the '55' in the top left-hand corner shows the depth of water, while the '0' and '60'on the right-hand side shows the range.

Auto range

All modern fishfinders have an automatic mode which, in most models, is activated when you switch on. In this mode the sounder will automatically locate and lock onto the sea bed, then continue to select the most appropriate range to keep the bottom in the lower half of the screen.

At the same time the sounder will automatically adjust the sensitivity so that the optimum signal is received. Some recent Lowrance/Eagle models with Advanced

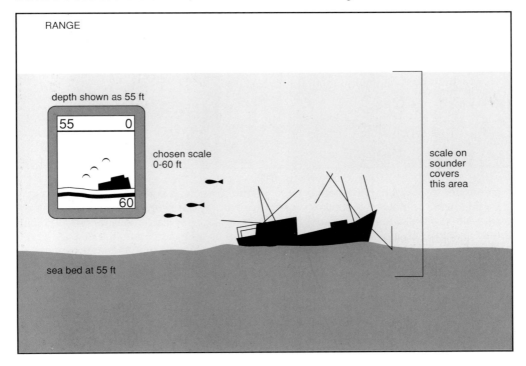

RANGE

depth shown as 55 ft

55   0

chosen scale
0-60 ft

60

scale on sounder covers this area

sea bed at 55 ft

Signal Processing (ASP) make other adjustments to counteract the effects of boatspeed and water interference.

Automatic mode is particularly helpful when you are starting out with your fishfinder, and of course when you want hands-free operation because you are busy with other activities on the boat. But sometimes it can be a disadvantage, particularly when the sea bed shows near the centre of the screen and the depth of water is not quite shallow enough to trigger the next range scale.

With some older models, using the automatic mode is not recommended in very shallow water because the surface clutter can extend to the bottom of the screen. The sounder cannot distinguish between the clutter and the sea bed, and has difficulty locking onto the bottom. Sounders fitted with Advanced Signal Processing (ASP) overcome this restriction. The automatic mode may also lose the bottom if it is sloping steeply, but if this happens the digital display will flash a warning to the operator.

Zoom, shift and bottom track

If you want to examine the sea bed or the area near the sea bed in more detail, you can switch to 'zoom'. On the left of the diagram below we are still in 55 feet of water, but we now have a zoom range of 30-60 feet displayed. The image is magnified by a factor of two, doubling the size of the echoes.

Many sounders also have the facility to move the zoom window up or down, so that if the depth of water changes, the bottom can be kept in the same place on the screen. This is known as 'shift'. On the right of the diagram below the bottom is now deeper at 62 feet; we have therefore shifted the zoom down five feet to display a zoom range of 35-65 feet.

In rapidly changing depth conditions it would be time-consuming to keep shifting the zoom around, so many sounders are equipped to do this automatically. This function is known as 'bottom tracking', 'auto-tracking', 'auto-shift' and, on some sounders, 'bottom lock' – although true bottom lock is slightly different.

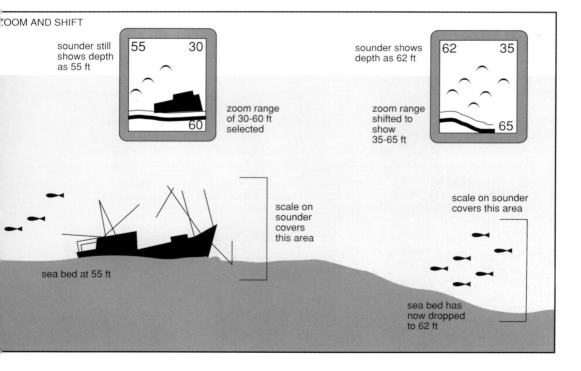

ZOOM AND SHIFT

sounder still shows depth as 55 ft

55   30

60

zoom range of 30-60 ft selected

sounder shows depth as 62 ft

62   35

65

zoom range shifted to show 35-65 ft

scale on sounder covers this area

scale on sounder covers this area

sea bed at 55 ft

sea bed has now dropped to 62 ft

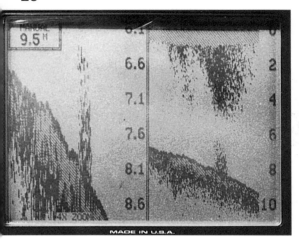

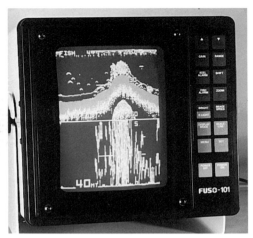

ABOVE **An obstruction on the sea bed displayed in zoom mode (left) and normal mode (right) on a split screen. Note that in zoom mode the image has been stretched vertically, because although the vertical dimension has been magnified the horizontal dimension has not.**

ABOVE **A Fuso colour video sounder in bottom lock mode. The upper section of the screen shows the normal surface-to-sea bed picture; the lower section shows the bottom lock facility, with the fish displayed above a straight line representing the sea bed.**

Split-screen

If you are using zoom mode you will often find yourself wondering if there is something interesting swimming around just above your upper depth setting. One way of checking is to use the the split-screen facility, a recent development that enables the sounder to display a surface-to-bottom picture on one side of the screen and a zoom picture on the other.

Bottom lock

Owners who have used a sounder at sea over a flat bottom will have noticed that the motion of the boat over the waves is mirrored by the appearance of a series of shark's-tooth 'waves' in the sea bed signal. This is a real problem to, say, a commercial fisherman towing a trawl in heavy weather to catch fish near the bottom, since he cannot see exactly where the fish are in relation to the sea bed.

To overcome this problem, manufacturers developed the 'bottom lock' facility which locks the sounder onto the bottom signal when it is in zoom or expanded-range mode. The sea bed is presented as a straight line, and an inverted scale

shows the distance above the bottom of any fish. Bottom lock is normally available only on colour video sounders, which often have a split-screen option to display the standard picture at the same time.

Range selection

On the older paper sounders, the range was generally selected by a four- six- or eight-position switch. Position 1 might give you a scale of 0-60 feet, position 2 a scale of 0-120 feet, and so on. Sometimes these scales were phased, so that the position 2 scale in this case would be 60-120 feet. Things were pretty simple then.

BELOW **The six-position range switch on a Fuji Royal paper sounder of the late 1970s.**

With the advent of video and particularly liquid crystal (LCG) sets, manufacturers began to incorporate calculator-type keypads that enabled the operator to enter any depth range or lower limit he wanted. He could also enter any upper limit. So if the operator wanted to examine an area extending just 15 feet above the sea bed at 55 feet, he could select a lower limit of 57 feet and an upper limit of 42 feet. Manufacturers refer to these sounders as having 'infinitely variable depth ranges'.

Obviously such machines are very versatile, but owing to their rather daunting appearance there has been a move away from this design concept, and many of the latest machines have a number of set depth ranges. These are selected using an on-screen menu – a list on the screen telling you which buttons to press to get your required function. The bottom half of each range can be expanded to cover the whole screen, to show 10-20 feet, 20-40 feet or whatever. This is described in the brochures as 'multiple zoom ranges'.

Incidentally, although some sounders are calibrated in both feet and metres, many are either just feet or just metres. If you have a strong preference, be sure to check this before purchasing. If you are going to use the unit in European waters, bear in mind that the depths on European charts are given in metres – so even if you prefer to think in feet it may be sensible to choose a metric sounder.

Depth alarm

All video and liquid crystal models (but not paper recording sounders) are equipped with one or more alarms that sound if the boat moves into water that is either shallower or deeper than a preset depth setting. The shallow alarm is obviously a useful safety aid to help prevent grounding. The deep alarm, if fitted, is useful as an anchor alarm, or when drifting to locate drop-offs and gullies.

Some models also have a zone alarm that sounds if an echo appears in a preset section of the screen. This is particularly useful when trolling or using a downrigger.

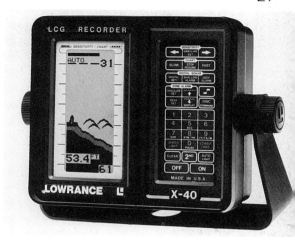

ABOVE **An early LCG; some 32 push buttons, some with two functions, made an operator's manual essential.**

Windows

This function is found only on the very latest models, and allows the operator to split the screen into two, three or four rectangles to show digital and chart information on the screen at the same time. Each rectangle or window can be adjusted individually by pressing the appropriate menu button, allowing access to the necessary controls or features.

BELOW **A basic menu selection system: pressing the button indicated by the on-screen label switches the unit into split-screen mode.**

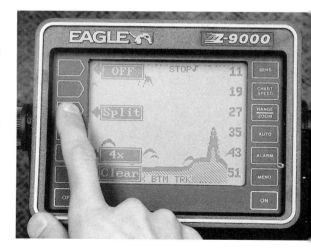

Menus

Most of the latest models, particularly those in the middle and higher price ranges, are controlled through on-screen menus. This makes them more user-friendly than the older models, because you are guided through the various functions by information on the screen. The operator's manual is hardly necessary.

On most sets there are a number of levels of information and operation. For example, a sounder may have a button marked 'zoom'. Press it and a menu appears, superimposed on top of the normal picture. Headed 'zoom size', the menu has zoom-up and zoom-down arrows related to buttons on the set. Touching and holding the relevant button changes the size of the zoom window, making it either larger or smaller. This is indicated by changing figures on the screen, and each change may be acknowledged by a bleep.

The menu box usually remains on the screen for a few seconds to allow any further adjustments, then automatically clears. Alternatively, you can delete it by pressing 'exit' or 'clear'.

BELOW **A Lowrance X-70 in windows mode, showing six pieces of information. On the left are digital readings of depth, water temperature, boatspeed and distance run; on the right are the graph recording and the battery voltage, displayed both digitally and as a bar graph.**

Other choices shown on the zoom menu could read '2x', '4x', 'split' or 'full'. This means that you can select a zoom picture which is twice or four times magnified, and portrayed on the full screen or on either half of a split screen, with the other half showing the full surface-to-bottom picture.

You can often obtain further information or choices by pushing the button next to the on-screen word 'more'.

Sensitivity

If you have purchased a liquid crystal fishfinder in the last couple of years, you will have adjusted the sensitivity and surface clutter controls very rarely, if at all, since modern sets make these adjustments automatically unless the automatic systems are overridden. If you have a paper sounder, however, or an older liquid crystal unit, you will have to master these controls since careful adjustment makes all the difference between finding or not finding fish.

The sensitivity or gain control is one of the most important controls on the sounder. It works rather like the volume control on a radio: the more you increase it, the more signal you allow into the set.

In shallow water you need to restrict the amount of signal received by the set, or it will display every piece of flotsam and water turbulence under the boat and the paper or screen will become covered in a mass of black interference. In deeper water, on the other hand, you will need the sensitivity turned up so that the set picks up the smaller targets – such as fish.

A quirk of this control is that the strength of signal received increases exponentially as you turn the knob. So by turning it from, say, the halfway position to the three-quarter position you may increase the sensitivity by ten or more times. This can be disconcerting until you get used to it.

The best way to adjust the sensitivity is to turn the knob until the paper or screen goes black, then very slowly reduce it so

ABOVE **If the sensitivity is too low – shown on the left by the narrow bottom signal – the sounder will not register fish.To show fish, increase the sensitivity to give light background speckling.**

that a light background speckling just appears; the fish will then show up clearly. Alternatively you could try a method used by commercial fishermen: select a scale of more than double the depth of water, then increase the sensitivity until a faint secondary bottom echo appears. This indicates the optimum sensitivity level.

Problems with paper sounders can often be traced back to poor adjustment of the sensitivity control. A few years ago I visited a customer who had recently purchased a paper sounder, and was complaining that although it showed a very nice profile of the bottom he had never seen a fish on it – even though he was catching them from under the boat. I watched him switch on the set and correctly turn up the sensitivity until the paper blackened. But then he yanked the control back to the halfway position: 'There,' he said after a few seconds, 'a good bottom, but no fish!'

I slowly eased the sensitivity knob around towards the three-quarter position and, although some light background speckling showed on the paper, we almost immediately started to see fish appearing as the familiar dots and blobs.

Surface clutter

The surface clutter control, – sometimes known as time variable gain (TVG) or sensitivity time control (STC) – is used to reduce on-screen interference caused by air bubbles and plankton in the top layer of water. This shows on a sounder as a band of black dots, and has the effect of blocking out fish signals near the surface.

The control works by suppressing the mass of very small interference signals that would otherwise be displayed in the upper part of the screen or paper, to leave only the larger marks that are most likely to be fish. The adjustment is critical – if you turn the knob too far you lose the fish as well.

Manufacturers' literature often suggests that this clutter only affects the top five or ten feet of the picture, but I have often seen 'curtains' of this clutter extending down to 40 or 50 feet, and on occasions blotting out the whole screen to even greater depths. At such times I have often been convinced that the set has developed a fault, but it is simply the effect of a local plankton bloom. On these occasions the clutter control has little effect, and the only thing to do is move a few yards to find clear water.

BELOW **The screen of an LCD unit showing the effect of the surface clutter control: switched on (left) to suppress the clutter, and switched off.**

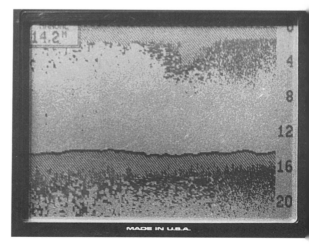

Advanced signal processing (ASP)

This is an automatic function that uses electronics to monitor various factors that affect the performance of a fishfinder – including boatspeed, water conditions and interference sources – and adjust the sensitivity, surface clutter and other settings to give the best picture quality.

MORE SOUNDER FUNCTIONS

All the important and commonly-used functions found on fishfinders have been described. This section examines some of the other controls and displays you may find on liquid crystal and video sets. Controls that are found only on paper recorders are described on page 48.

Fastrak

This function is also variously known as Adscope, A-scope and Fishlupe.

Normally the echoes from each incoming pulse show on the display along a single vertical line of pixels, starting on the far right-hand side of the screen and scrolling across to the left to build an image of the bottom and fish. When

Fastrak is switched on, these incoming pulses are expanded horizontally to cover several vertical lines of pixels, forming a bar that may cover about a quarter of the width of the screen. On some models the whole screen is used.

By this means, each incoming fish echo is stretched to show as a horizontal line. This can be identified more quickly, and its exact depth can be measured more accurately. The thickness of the line gives an instant indication of the strength of the echo, and on video sounders its size and colour helps to identify the fish species. This function is particularly useful at anchor, when the fish echoes can be long drawn out and the standard graph can appear confusing.

Three-beam Fastrak

Similar to the standard Fastrak, the latest three-dimensional models can offer the facility to simultaneously magnify the incoming trains of pulses from three transducer beams, giving a fan-like picture of the water under the boat. This enables you to see the depth of the fish easily, their actual position, and the bottom contours relative to the boat.

BELOW **This split screen has a Fastrak display to the right of the normal display. The returns are shown as blocks in a column next to a depth scale to make depth assessment easier.**

BELOW **A three-beam Fastrak displays block-style returns from three transducers at once to give a more comprehensive picture of the water under the boat.**

Chart cursor

This is a thin horizontal line extending across the display which can be moved up and down. When it is located over a specific echo the exact depth of the target is shown as a digital readout in a small box. Some sets are equipped with a log, and these may feature a cross-hair cursor that shows the depth of the target and its distance behind the boat.

Battery back-up

A few of the more expensive models are equipped with small lithium batteries that have a lifespan of several years. Such a battery enables the set to remember the last settings used before switch-off. This means that the unit requires a minimum of setting-up when it is switched on again in similar waters or fishing conditions. The back-up function can be disabled on some models if required.

Memory

When you are making a search of the sea bed it is sometimes useful to compare the information on the screen with a previously-recorded picture. Accordingly some sounders have the facility to memorise and store up to four screens of information, and these can then be displayed at a later date.

On some of the very latest top-range models the information can be downloaded into a computer. This feature is particularly handy if you want to show your friends the size of the one that got away!

Reverse scroll

This function uses the memory to pull the last screen of information back onto the display for comparative purposes.

Keel offset

On larger boats and yachts the keel may be several feet deeper than the transducer. This control allows that distance to be programmed into the sounder so that the depth of water is shown from the keel, and not from the transducer.

Preset

Pressing this key clears the programme and makes the sounder revert to the settings it had when brand new and fresh out of the box. This is useful for quickly clearing a complex or forgotten programme. If you have a combined echo-sounder and GPS navigator system, however, the navigator may have to be set up again from scratch if this you activate this control.

Contrast

This control alters the contrast between the image and the background, and may need adjusting to suit the light conditions.

Species select

This facility is found on some of the Bottom Line range of sounders for use only in the USA. These have been pre-programmed with information about the habitat of certain species, and when the information is recalled the machine automatically selects a suitable combination of settings for locating those particular fish.

5 TECHNICAL SPECIFICATIONS ·················

Study any fishfinder brochure and you will find the manufacturer boasting of high-resolution displays, wide beam angles and high power output. Look in the technical specification columns and you will find references to frequency and pulse length. But what does it all mean?

Beam angle

The beam angle or beam width is simply the angle of the cone-shaped path followed by the ultrasonic energy pulse. In fact the pulse of energy is not transmitted in an exact cone, but it is described in this way for the sake of simplicity.

The diagram below shows a beam angle of 20 degrees – i.e. 10 degrees either side of the vertical line to produce a 20-degree cone. If you increase the beam angle to, say, 36 or even the 60 degrees available on some models, you get a greater area of coverage under the boat,

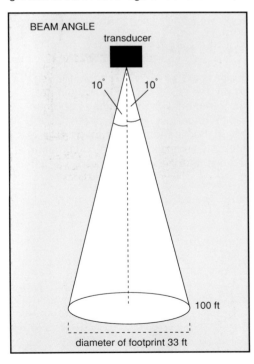

BEAM ANGLE

transducer

10° 10°

100 ft

diameter of footprint 33 ft

but reduced maximum depth penetration. Conversely if you decrease the beam angle to 8-10 degrees, the concentration of the beam increases maximum depth penetration at the expense of coverage.

As a rough rule of thumb, the diameter of the circular footprint painted on the bottom by a 60-degree beam is about the same as the depth. So in 100 feet of water a 60-degree beam will cover an area 100 feet across, a 20-degree beam will cover an area about 33 feet across (a third of the depth), and an eight-degree beam will cover an area about 16 feet across (a sixth of the depth)

Power output

Power output is measured in watts – 200W or so for the lower-power models, rising to 3000W for the high-power units. Most manufacturers use a measurement called peak-to-peak, but do check if you are comparing models because some brochures give the root-mean-square figure (RMS), which is one eighth of the peak-to-peak figure.

The higher the power output, the greater the depth penetration of the sounder, and the greater its ability to see smaller fish at depth.

Frequency, pulse length and resolution

Most sports fishing sounders operate at a frequency of around 200 kHz. This means that they transmit their pulses at 200,000 cycles per second. They are known as high-frequency sounders.

Many commercial sounders are low-frequency units, transmitting their pulse at 50 kHz (or 50,000 cycles per second). This frequency allows them to see fish at much greater depths than their high-frequency counterparts, and to get better ground discrimination (GD) performance. In other words, since the lower-frequency pulse suffers less attenuation on its journey through the water, it gives better-quality secondary bottom echoes to enable operators to see, at a glance, the difference between a hard and soft sea bed. The generally wider beam also enhances GD performance.

Unfortunately, low-frequency sounders also have low resolution, because they transmit long pulses of energy that cannot resolve targets that are close together and display them as separate echoes. So if two fish are swimming close together a low-frequency sounder will display them as one mark on the screen, whereas a high-frequency unit operating on a shorter pulse length will be able to resolve those fish into two separate marks. Furthermore, while fish swimming just above the sea bed will show up on a high-frequency unit, they will merge into the sea bed signal on a low-frequency sounder. 50 kHz receivers also tend to give a rather coarse picture, particularly in shallow water. These disadvantages are generally ignored by commercial fisherman, who are normally interested only in large

schools in deep water. Anglers and other sports users, however, prefer higher-frequency machines that are able to discriminate small echoes in shallower depths.

Different depths of water require different pulse lengths for optimum performance. As we have seen, a long pulse length will give greater depth penetration than a short pulse, and both high and low frequency sounders are designed to automatically switch to longer pulses as deeper ranges are selected.

A few sounders permit the operator to manually change the pulse length. The unit may offer a choice of short, medium or long or, in the case of one or two of the advanced paper recorders, to a length determined by the operator. Some of the older paper recorders, such as the Eagle Mach 1 and Mach 2, also had a suppressor control that could be adjusted to increase the pulse length, which offered two benefits: it gave better performance in deep water, and it had the effect of rejecting interference, which is normally received as short pulses of energy.

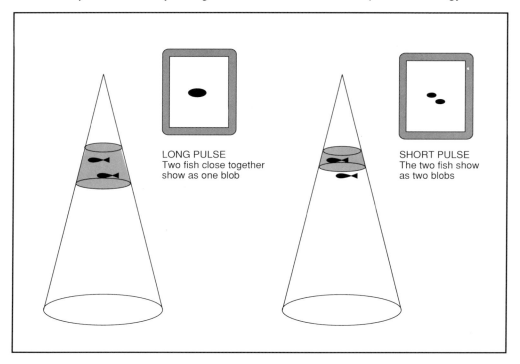

LONG PULSE
Two fish close together show as one blob

SHORT PULSE
The two fish show as two blobs

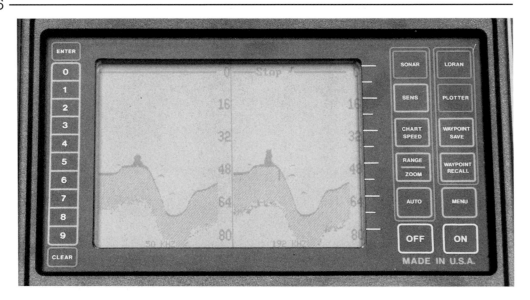

ABOVE **A split-screen LCD with a low resolution 50 kHz picture on the left and a high-resolution 192 kHz picture on the right.**

Sometimes you need to select a short pulse length. Some years ago, I arranged a demonstration of a Lowrance X15A paper recorder to a biologist who needed to know the height of some dense weed growth above the bottom of a shallow lake. On a shallow range scale that used a factory-set pulse length, the sounder could not penetrate the top of the weed growth. The weed showed up as the bottom, as we proved with the aid of a long pole. But when we selected the very shortest pulse length available the machine was able both to discriminate the individual fonds of weed, and penetrate that weed to display the actual bottom.

Choosing the optimum specification

You will often be advised to buy the highest power sounder you can afford. This is generally true, but you should balance this against your specific requirements – particularly if the machine is only going to be used in shallow water.

There is little point in buying a 3000-watt sounder if it is only going to be used on a freshwater lake less than 60 feet

deep. A 300-watt model would be quite adequate. However, a more expensive model would probably offer better screen resolution, and the facility to manually shorten the pulse length to improve discrimination. For shallow-water use, link the sounder to a transducer with a wide beam of not less than a 20 degrees.

For fishing at sea in up to 200 feet of water, you should look for a machine with at least 600 watts of power, and link it to a transducer with a beamwidth of around 20 degrees. In even deeper water you should consider a narrower, eight-degree beamwidth transducer.

A high-power sounder will certainly not be wasted at sea in any depths over 100 feet, where it will pick up smaller fish at far deeper depths than a low-power model. The really high power sounders can show the sea bed at depths of more than 500 feet if used with a wide-beam transducer, and more than 1000 feet with a narrow-beam transducer. Incidentally, a sounder's performance is always better in fresh water, because there is less suspended material to attenuate the pulse.

If you intend using the unit at all depths, you could fit both a narrow- and wide-beam transducer in the boat, and select them via a changeover switch.

Screen resolution

Confusingly, the word resolution has two meanings: as well as describing the sounder's ability to discern details underwater, the term is also used to describe the number of lines or dots on the screen.

These dots are called pixels, which is short for picture elements. A sounder with a high-resolution display has many dots, up to 64,000 in the case of the top-range models, which are virtually indiscernible to give a smooth picture presentation. A low-resolution display has few dots, perhaps under 5000, giving a rather blocky or 'staircase' effect to the picture.

As we have seen, the result of each pulse is displayed on the screen as a vertical line of pixels, so if the screen is to display the fish and bottom in maximum detail, it must have as many vertical pixels as possible. Top-range sets have some 200, while mid-range sets have 125 to 150. The number of horizontal pixels is less important, since a wider screen simply gives more historical information. This is why some of the early liquid crystal models were manufactured with tall narrow screens rather than short wide ones.

The area of water represented by each pixel increases with depth because the display covers a larger volume of water,

ABOVE **A low-resolution display on an early LCG unit, with some 82 vertical and 32 horizontal pixels. The small total of 2624 pixels gives a rather 'blocky' presentation.**

so only screens with high vertical resolution are able to separate targets that are close together. For instance, a fish swimming just off the bottom will be shown as a separate echo on a high-resolution screen, but will merge with the bottom signal on a low-resolution display.

HOW MUCH WATER DOES ONE PIXEL REPRESENT?

RANGE	PIXEL AREA (82 VERTICAL PIXEL DISPLAY)	PIXEL AREA (192 VERTICAL PIXEL DISPLAY)
0 – 10 feet	1.5 inches	0.6 inches
0 – 20 feet	3 inches	1.5 inches
0 – 30 feet	4.5 inches	1.8 inches
0 – 40 feet	6 inches	2.5 inches
0 – 50 feet	7.5 inches	3.13 inches
0 – 60 feet	9 inches	3.75 inches
0 – 70 feet	10.5 inches	4.4 inches
0 – 80 feet	12.5 inches	5 inches
0 – 90 feet	14 inches	5.6 inches
0 – 100 feet	15.5 inches	6.25 inches

6 HOW FISH ARE DISPLAYED ····················

It is no coincidence that most of the world's sports fishfinder manufacturers are based in the USA. They are supported by a very active inland sports fishing market that has grown up around the many large freshwater lakes in America. A lot of these were deliberately created for recreational use shortly after the war when land was cheap. Because of this large inland market, American sounders tend to be promoted for lake fishing by their manufacturers, and the glossy brochures show the sort of results which can be expected under such conditions. This brings us to the problem of fish arches.

Many owners who take their newly-acquired sounders to sea are disappointed not to see large fish arches on the screen, as depicted in the brochure. In fact they often do not realise that the dots, squiggles and blobs that they do see represent the very fish they are searching for.

So are the brochures wrong? Not at all. If the boat is moving slowly over a large fish or shoal in flat, calm water, of the type usually found only on an inland lake, the fish signal will show as an arch. As the leading edge of the cone hits the fish the trace starts to form on the screen. As the boat passes over the fish, the distance between boat and fish decreases; as a result the trace is indicated at a shallower depth on the display, forming half the arch, and because the signal is stronger, the thickness of the trace increases. The full arch is formed on the display as the boat moves away from the fish, resulting in a deeper trace being recorded on the screen. From this it can be deduced that the actual depth of the fish is represented by the top of the arch.

But even in calm water the arches do not always show. Very small fish rarely arch, and in shallow water, say down to 20 feet, the beam will be too narrow to generate an arched signal. If the fish only passes through the edge of the beam it will not be in the cone long enough for the full arch to form, although some arching will take place, depending on the fish's

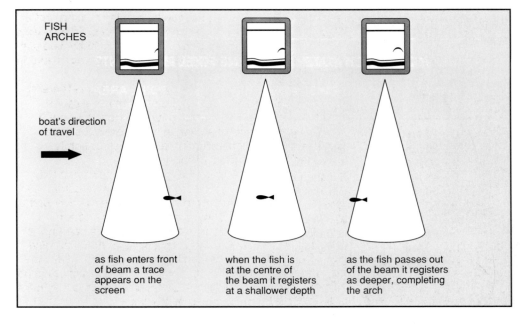

FISH ARCHES

boat's direction of travel

as fish enters front of beam a trace appears on the screen

when the fish is at the centre of the beam it registers at a shallower depth

as the fish passes out of the beam it registers as deeper, completing the arch

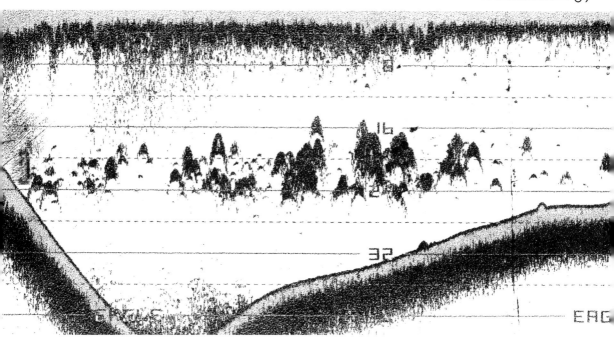

ABOVE **A paper trace of a freshwater lake, showing classic fish arches.**

BELOW **Fish contacts at sea, with a small shoal showing on the far left at a depth of 9.5 metres, and a fish or two on the right at 10.8 metres.**

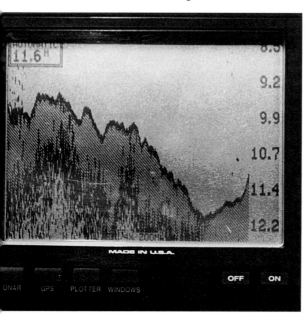

distance from the centre of the beam. Remember that the boat must be moving for arching to take place.

So why are these arches rarely seen at sea? The reason is the wave motion, which makes the boats pitch and roll. The beam is constantly moving around under the boat, so the fish are never in the beam long enough for the arch to build. you simply get a series of dots as the fish move in and out of the beam.

Even in fairly calm conditions there is often a swell at sea that prevents the arches forming fully. Instead you get a sort of squiggle, or a more substantial blob indicating a large fish or tightly-packed shoal.

Fish arches cannot be formed if the boat is drifting with the tide, because the fish will be drifting along on the tide with you. They may be under the boat for some time, in which case the screen will show a long squiggly line. If you are fishing at anchor, a stationary fish – like your hook – will be displayed as a line covering the full width of the screen since it is in the same place all the time.

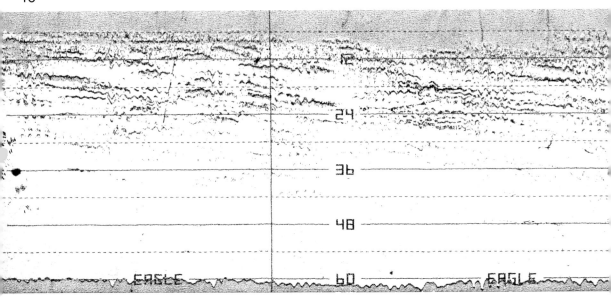

ABOVE **A shoal of mackerel detected by an Eagle Mach 1 paper recording sounder. Since the boat and fish were drifting at a similar speed each fish stayed in the transducer beam for some time, producing long traces.**

BELOW **A paper trace of a lake, showing a clear thermocline at a depth of 36 feet. Notice how the fish are concentrated in the thermocline zone.**

The thermocline

Sometimes, especially if you increase the sensitivity, you may detect a fuzzy band somewhere between the bed of a lake and a few feet below the surface. This is an indication of a thermocline: a boundary between two water masses of different

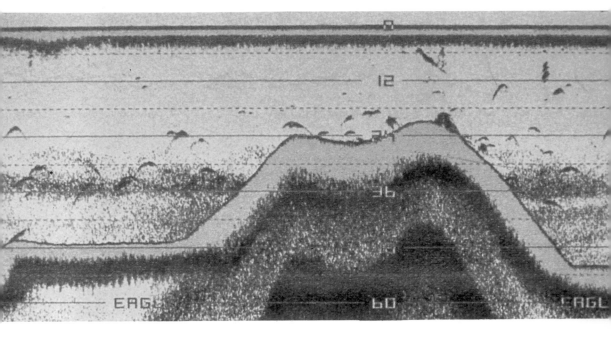

temperatures. It is displayed because the two bodies of water are of slightly different densities. In fresh water, particularly, fish often feed around this zone, so the phenomenon can be used to advantage by lake fishermen.

IDENTIFICATION OF FISH SPECIES

Many commercial fishermen using paper recorders and colour sounders can identify different species of fish by the shape, size and colour of the echoes displayed on the screen. This is a skill obtained through years of experience at interpreting the signals, assisted by a certain amount of local knowledge about fish stocks and their movements. It is doubtful whether any information of this type could be published in a meaningful way for general consumption.

Fish I.D. and alarm

All liquid crystal sounders now have a fish identification (I.D.) function which displays fish as fish shapes on the screen – often in three or four different sizes to reflect the size of the echo. When I first saw this I was inclined to dismiss it as a bit of a gimmick, but many users find it a most helpful way of isolating fish from background noise.

A word of warning, though. The processor is simply programmed to select echoes of predetermined sizes between the surface and sea bed and depict them as fish. It cannot, in fact, tell the difference between fish and lumps of seaweed and other submerged flotsam, and I would not recommend using this function if you want to get the very best from your machine, since it does not allow you to interpret the signals.

All modern sounders come equipped with a fish alarm. This sounds an audible alarm when a fish comes into the beam. Some models employ a different tone to indicate different sizes of fish, so it gets quite musical sometimes when the boat is going over a shoal.

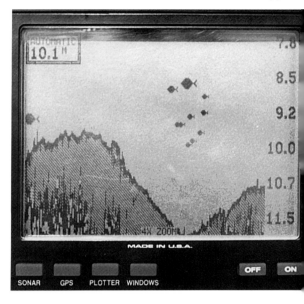

ABOVE **The effect of fish I.D. on a liquid crystal screen. The 'fish' are just symbols, however, representing isolated echoes; the actual objects may not be fish at all.**

FISH DETECTION PROBLEMS

The physical properties of the beam angle and the contours of the sea bed can sometimes conspire to make fish undetectable.

The dead zone

We have seen how the sounder transmits a cone-shaped pulse which bounces off the sea bed as a circular footprint, returning to the display to be processed as a scrolling picture on the screen. The information from the centre of the footprint, which is normally closest to the transducer, arrives first and is printed as the top edge of the sea bed trace on the display, with the rest of the footprint progressively thickening the trace as it is processed microseconds later.

This means that if there is a fish near the bottom at the centre of the footprint, it will be seen because its echo arrives back at the display before the bottom signal. But if the fish is slightly off-centre it will be

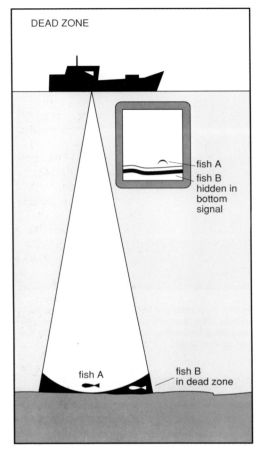

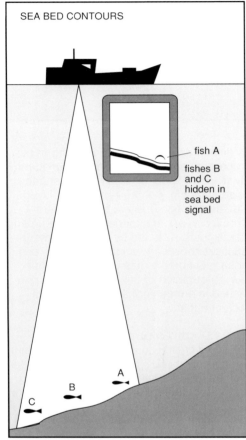

hidden by the stronger central bottom echo arriving to be processed by the display at the same time. As a result of this there is a saucer-shaped area within the bottom footprint where fish cannot be detected by the sounder. This is known as the dead zone.

Fish hidden by sea bed contours

If the sea bed is sloping the pulses describe an oval, elongated footprint, and this is displayed as a wider bottom signal on the screen. Fish lower down the slope have to be progressively higher off the bottom to be displayed by the sounder, because the stronger bottom signals from the higher part of the slope arrive at the same time as the fish echoes lower down the slope and mask them.

Similarly, if the sea bed is rocky with small gullies, fish on or near the bottom in the gullies will be lost in the stronger bottom signals being reflected from the higher ground.

Fish without swim bladders

Some of the older low-frequency echo sounders will only register fish with swim bladders. This is because the swim bladder contains air, and the sounder detects the difference in density between the air and the water. Because of this it is often thought that a fish such as a mackerel – which has no swim bladder – cannot be detected. However, all modern high-frequency fishfinders will pick up the sound pulse reflected from the body of the fish, so this is no longer a problem.

A three-dimensional fishfinder works in a similar way to a conventional sounder, but presents a picture that shows both the actual position of fish relative to the boat, and the contours of the bottom to either side of the boat's direction of travel.

The image is presented in the form of a cube, viewed from above the front left-hand corner. The boat's position is at the top centre of the leading edge of the cube, travelling towards the right, with the rest of the display showing the water and bottom that the boat has already passed over. Just like the conventional sounder, the picture is built up slice by slice, and scrolled to form the image.

A three-dimensional sounder is installed in exactly the same way as a conventional unit, except that the transducer must be more accurately mounted – either on the transom, or through the hull – so as to point vertically downward. In-hull mounting is not recommended because the edges of the very wide, fan-like beam would have to pass through a considerably greater thickness of the hull material than the centre of the beam. This

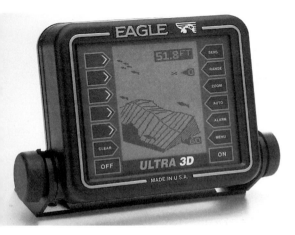

BELOW **An Eagle Ultra 3D. The boat's position is shown as the 'X' and arrowed by the 'O' mark over the centre line of the bottom contour.**

would give an uneven signal which would adversely affect the quality of the picture.

The transducer is larger than usual. This is because it is designed to transmit up to five pulses in quick succession, all at slightly different angles, in order to build up the three-dimensional image. The combined beam angle is about 60 degrees.

A speed sensor may be included with the installation kit. This enables the boat's speed to be shown on the display, and also permits the sounder to compute the distance between the front and the back of the bottom image, displaying the result as a digital read-out.

These displays have a number of advantages over conventional systems. The precise position of fish relative to both the boat and bottom can be seen – particularly if the fish ID mode is used, which paints a vertical line beneath each fish echo to show its exact location and height above the bottom. The contours of the bottom can be seen at a glance, as can the position, relative to the boat, of underwater objects such as wrecks.

A disadvantage is that some of the sets are limited in their range, showing depths to only 100 or 120 feet. More seriously, you cannot interpret the image on the screen for yourself, either to discern different bottom conditions and structure, or to detect small changes in the bottom make-up. However, this shortcoming has been partly overcome by Eagle with the three-beam Fastrak feature, which incorporates the greyline function.

Another problem is that these sets do not work well at speed, partly because of the increased water turbulence under the transducer, and partly because the transducer's angle to the water changes as the boat comes onto the plane, causing a 'pyramiding' effect on the picture. The bottom image also has a rather blocky, slab-sided look. Doubtless future developments will iron out these shortcomings.

8 SPEED, DISTANCE & WATER TEMPERATURE

Many fishfinders are now sold with a log, or with the option of fitting one. The word 'log' can be used to describe an instrument giving either speed or distance, and is derived from a sixteenth-century device comprising a triangular piece of wood, or log, that was thrown overboard, attached to a length of thin rope knotted at regular intervals. The time taken for a given number of knots to run out was measured, and from this the speed could be calculated. Hence the speed of a ship is normally expressed in knots.

A knot is one nautical mile per hour, and a nautical mile represents one minute of latitude. Although the length of a minute of latitude does vary slightly between the equator and the poles, a standardised length of 6080 feet or 1852 metres is used by mariners. A knot is the equivalent of 1.151 statute miles per hour.

In the USA a large number of sports fishing sounders are used on inland waters, and for this reason some American units are calibrated to give speed and distance in statute miles and miles per hour. If the sounder has an optional metric scale switching to this will often adjust the log calibration to knots and nautical miles. Most Japanese makes use the nautical scale. So if you require an integral log as part of your sounder, check that your choice of model is calibrated in an acceptable scale.

Installation

Owners of small craft now have a choice of several different types of log, including electromagnetic, pressure, doppler and paddlewheel devices. The paddlewheel type seems to be preferred by sounder manufacturers because of its simplicity of design and ability to give unambiguous readings. It consists of a small paddle that rotates in a housing, triggering a signal with every full rotation; the faster the boat travels the faster the paddle spins. The signal is transmitted via a cable to the sounder unit, where it is processed to give a reading on the screen.

It is important that the paddlewheel is accessible to enable seaweed and other flotsam to be removed. In yachts and larger craft the paddlewheel is mounted in a skin fitting that can be withdrawn through a hole in the hull, using a blanking plug to stop water getting in while the wheel is being cleaned. This can also be used if the vessel is liable to ground.

On small craft and fast planing boats it is usual to fit a lightweight paddlewheel by simply screwing it to the outside of the transom. There is then no need to drill a large hole in the hull. Ideally it should be fitted to one side of the centreline so that the paddle is just below the hull.

A transom paddlewheel is ideal for small outboard-powered craft – not only because of the ease of installation, but also because the base of the transom is often the only part of the boat in a good solid lump of water. So, as with the sounder transducer, it is only here that an accurate reading can be obtained.

Sometimes the paddlewheel is integral with the depth transducer and a water

BELOW **A transom-mounted paddlewheel log transducer. The temperature sensor is the small metal insert.**

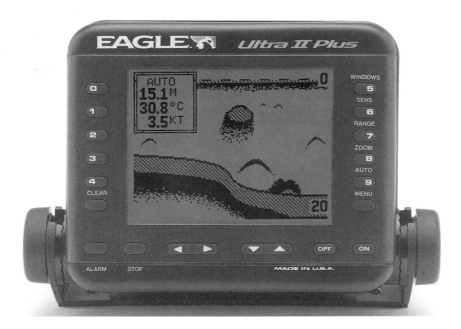

temperature sensor, and such a fitting is called a triducer. Triducers can be either through-hull or transom-mounted.

ABOVE **An Eagle Ultra II Plus in metric mode, showing the depth in metres, water temperature in degrees celsius and speed in knots.**

Accuracy
It is important to understand that the log only gives the speed and distance travelled *through the water*, and not over the ground. If, for example, your boat was travelling at five knots against a three-knot tide your log would read five knots – whereas in reality you would only be making good only two knots over the ground. So you should have a tidal stream atlas that shows the speed and direction of the tides for calculating ETAs at sea. Tidal information can also be found on charts.

As the boat moves through the water it creates friction. This has the effect of dragging a thin layer of water along with the boat, so if the log sensor is operating in this thin layer – and it usually is – the log will not show the correct reading.

Although the effect is normally slight on small craft, some sounders have a calibration facility to allow for it. The calibration must be carried out over a measured distance; normally a mile. Measured miles can be found marked on some charts, and the calibration should be made after a timed run in both directions to negate any effect of wind and tide. Slack water is the ideal time for these runs. In fact few sounders have a log calibration facility, and normally the factory settings are accurate to within a few per cent.

Water temperature
Water temperature readouts are also available on many models, using either a sensor combined with the depth or speed transducers, or a small probe or plate screwed to the transom below the waterline. Water temperature information is used much more widely in the USA than in the Europe. In the Gulf Stream area off the Florida coast, for example, marked variations in sea temperature can occur only a short distance apart, so totally different species of fish can be found if the sounder operator has the facility to determine the water temperature.

9 PAPER RECORDERS ·······························

Unlike liquid crystal and video sounders; paper recorders are built with a number of moving parts, and include two electric motors – one to drive the stylus belt, and the other to operate the paper drive mechanism through a reduction gearbox. These moving parts mean that any paper recorder is inherently less reliable than a solid state echo sounder, although with a little careful maintenance it should operate fault-free for many years. The recorder will also need regular reloading with paper.

MAINTENANCE

Each time the stylus moves over the paper it releases a small quantity of black carbon dust which gives off a characteristic smell (which, incidentally, I have not found helpful to seasickness in rough water). This dust must be cleaned out after every four or five rolls of paper, or it will accumulate and cloud the inside of the perspex front window, clog the gearbox and interfere with the other machinery. A small, stiff paintbrush is the most useful tool for removing this accumulation from the gears, and a cloth soaked in a little methylated spirit is ideal for cleaning the inside of the case and polishing the perspex door.

The stylus should be checked for wear, and renewed when appropriate – ideally after every two or three rolls. The stylus is usually a U-shaped piece of wire held onto the stylus belt by a frame. As the belt moves down it drags one leg of the stylus over a metal plate, called the signal transfer brush, picking up the electrical signal from each received pulse and conducting it across to the other leg to be marked on

BELOW **The Eagle Mach 1 – the best and most popular chart recorder ever produced for small boat use.**

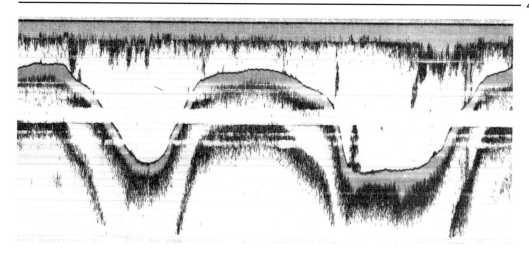

the moving paper. The stylus legs sometimes need to be bent slightly to maintain good contacts. Some models such as the Fuji Royals have a two-part stylus which fits on either side of a small bar across the belt, but it operates in the same way.

If you get a band of unmarked paper, this is a sign that the stylus belt is worn. This is called belt skip, and the only remedy is to replace the belt. Most sports users only need to do this every couple of years. The rubber wheels that the belt rides on should also be cleaned occasionally with a little meths.

If the noise level is higher than normal, or even a high-pitched screech, this usually indicates a worn gear in the paper drive gearbox. Often a very small dab of car grease will reduce the problem. On the Eagle Mach 1 and Mach 2 the culprit is usually the very smallest gear attached to the drive motor.

Do not be tempted to spray the inside of the machine with a water repellent such as WD40, since this can damage some of the components.

Carry out any maintenance with the power off, since you risk electric shock owing to the high voltages in the machine. Incidentally some of the early American recorders with metal cases were not isolated, and I have heard reports of users suffering electric shocks simply by touching the outside of the case in wet weather.

Finally on the subject of maintenance, it is important that the recorder is stored in an upright position so that any moisture caused by condensation can drain out through the small holes in the bottom of the case. If it is left on its back, condensation will collect on the printed circuit board and lead to corrosion.

PAPER LOADING

Before fitting a new roll of paper, make sure you move the stylus back behind the paper drive assembly to avoid damaging it. The paper roll is held on shafts, and is fed across the display between two spools rather like the film in a camera. On most recorders you load the new roll onto the right-hand shaft nearest the stylus belt, taking care that the spool engages on a notched key on the shaft base. You then pull the end across the face of the metal plate, known as the platen, and feed it around a roller to the take-up spool, where it is attached either by a piece of tape or by inserting a tapered end into a slot in the spool. On most units the old spool from a used roll has to be retained and moved to the other spindle, where it becomes the take-up spool.

ABOVE **The effect of wraparound: a secondary bottom echo appearing between the surface and the bottom signal. In this example, obtained during a survey of Loch Ness in Scotland, the water was some 220 metres deep and the secondary echo has been recorded as a faint band at just below 50 metres.**

Normally you then rotate the take-up spool to tension the paper. Clipping a sprung bar or hinged latch over the top of the spools holds them firmly in position.

One some of the later models the whole paper drive assembly is in the form of a removable cartridge. The cartridges themselves are loaded in much the same way as the paper on a conventional machine, but once made up they are much easier to load into the recorder, particularly at sea in rough weather.

Having loaded the machine or cartridge, check that the paper is the right way round. The coated surface should be facing outwards, or the stylus will not be able to mark it. If in doubt, run a fingernail across it – a mark will appear on the coated surface, but not on the reverse side.

Finally, carefully replace the paper drive assembly, or cartridge, back in the case and close the door. Switch on and run the paper at full speed for a second or two to take up any slack in the paper.

PAPER RECORDER CONTROLS

Many of the switches on paper recorders control and activate exactly the same functions as those on liquid crystal and video models: sensitivity, range and white/grey line, for example. But several functions are found only on paper recorders.

Paper speed
As the name suggests, this switch alters the speed at which the paper moves under the stylus. A slow paper speed may conserve paper, but it will also reduce the detail of the picture. A fast paper speed

will give a better-quality picture, and in particular will give clearer fish signals.

In deeper water, the paper speed will automatically slow down because the sound pulse takes longer to reach the sea bed and return.

Marker button

Depressing this control produces a continuous line on the paper. This is useful, both for noting times and positions of interesting marks, and also for checking that the stylus is making continuous contact with the paper.

Zero adjust

Sometimes, after replacing a paper roll, stylus or stylus belt, the whole picture may slip slightly on the chart. This can be corrected using the zero adjust function, which takes the form of a rotating knob or a simple slide control.

Alternate transmit and print

In very deep water you may encounter both overprint and wraparound on your sounder.

When the paper is moving very slowly, the stylus may print over the previous line of information to some extent, resulting in a very heavy black picture. This is called overprint.

In deep water secondary bottom echoes can be a nuisance because they may appear in the top or middle of the picture above the true bottom, and interfere with fish signals. This is because the secondary signals have taken so long to return from the bottom that the stylus has completed its circuit around the back of the paper and is already printing the next line of information when the processing and marking of the secondary echoes occurs. This is called wraparound.

The alternate transmit and print control prevents both these problems by triggering the pulse every second revolution of the stylus. The stylus prints a line of information on the paper, but on the next revolution it prints nothing. So the paper moves further between each marking run of the stylus, preventing overprint, and the time delay between pulses mean that the late secondary echoes do not register.

The alternate print and transmit mode can also reduce the interference from plankton and air bubbles in the water, known as reverberation, which sometimes occurs in low-frequency models. Some paper saving is also possible when using this function.

Position information

A few top-range paper recorders such as the Lowrance X16 sounder have the facility to print out position information if they are interfaced with a Loran C or GPS navigator.

10 INTERFERENCE ··································

One of the most irritating problems that you may encounter with any new sounder is interference – either from other electronic equipment on the boat or from water turbulence.

ELECTRICAL INTERFERENCE

Interference from other electronic devices is displayed as a series of short vertical lines or dots, giving the screen a grainy or dirty appearance.

Careful running of power leads and transducer cables will usually prevent this problem. Unfortunately most boat owners like to tidy such cabling away together in conduit, and this encourages radiated energy to pass directly from one cable to to another. It is important to keep the cables separate, particularly those that carry high-energy signals to transducers and VHF aerials.

Interference can also be caused by binding power cables together, or using a single cable from the battery to a junction box distributing power to the electronics. Persistent problems can sometimes be cured by running separate cables to the battery from equipment, or even using a second battery dedicated to the sounder or VHF.

If the interference only occurs when the outboard is running, fit suppressed, or low resistance plugs. If this fails, try lining the engine cowling with tin foil.

Other electrical gear can also interfere with your electronics. I had a customer who was sure his Decca navigator reacted to different meteorological conditions because it suffered from a high noise level when it was raining! As you might guess, the problem was traced to interference from the windscreen wiper motor. Cabin lights, navigation lights and bilge pumps can also generate noise. You can buy interference filters which may help.

Many manufacturers have boosted the output power of their machines in the quest for greater fishfinding capabilities, and this can greatly increase the amount of radiation being emitted from the display. This particularly affects VHF radios which, if mounted in close proximity to the sounder, can amplify the pulses so they sound as a rapid clicking noise from the loudspeaker. Although positioning these instruments as far away from each other as possible will reduce the problem, it is an unfortunate fact that no amount of position juggling will significantly reduce the nuisance from some of the most powerful top-range models. Turning down the squelch control on the radio is often the only way to deal with the problem.

WATER INTERFERENCE

The other type of interference that affects fishfinders is caused by air bubbles in the flow of water along the hull. This type of interference is characterised by a good bottom picture when the boat is stationary, but the image progressively breaks up as the boat moves faster through the water. It is particularly pronounced at the bows, where highly aerated water is produced as the boat cuts through the waves, so the transducer should never be installed in the bow area except for trolling at low speeds. Rubbing strakes or other protrusions from the hull may have the same effect, so avoid mounting the transducer anywhere near such obstructions.

INTERFERENCE SUPPRESSION

Assuming the installation is as good as you can get it, but you still suffer interference, how can you reduce its effect?

Most of the modern American liquid crystal sounders can filter out all but the

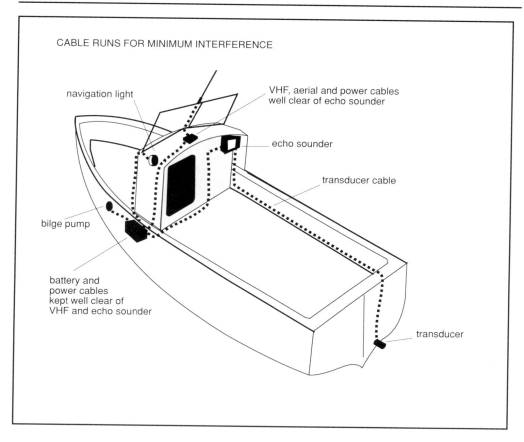

CABLE RUNS FOR MINIMUM INTERFERENCE

navigation light

VHF, aerial and power cables
well clear of echo sounder

echo sounder

transducer cable

bilge pump

battery and
power cables
kept well clear of
VHF and echo sounder

transducer

worst electrical noise with automatic noise rejection circuits, and the most recent Lowrance and Eagle models also have Advanced Signal Processing, another automatic function that rejects much of the interference caused by water turbulence.

But if you have an older sounder, or a paper recorder, what then? A number of these models have a suppression control which, when adjusted, will increase the length of the pulse transmitted by the machine. Since most noise pulses are short, they will be rejected as this control is advanced. However, increasing the pulse length results in a coarser signal, and this reduces the sounder's ability to discern individual fish that are close together or near the bottom.

Some of the Lowrance models also had a discrimination control – a patented device for eliminating random noise gen-

erated by interference without affecting the pulse length. The sounder processes the vertical lines of pixels, comparing each to the previous line. If an echo appears in the same place, it is displayed. If not, as in the case of random interference, it is rejected. The function can be set at a number of levels to increase the number of times an echo has to be received in the same place before it is displayed.

Many of the Japanese models are equipped with a similar control called fine echo or clean echo, which do much the same job.

All these functions can help, but the key to avoiding interference is to get the installation right, with a good transducer position and clear cable and wiring runs. The vast majority of owners have no problems at all with their sounders once they are installed.

11 USING FISHFINDERS IN FRESH WATER ······

In the USA, freshwater anglers are among the main customers for fishfinders – indeed many American units have been specifically designed to meet their needs. In the UK and Europe the situation is quite different. Talk to any sea angler with his own boat, and you will find that if he doesn't own a fishfinder already, it is certainly on his shopping list. Have the same conversation with a coarse fisherman, and you would be lucky to find one in a hundred who was even considering getting one.

At first sight there may appear to be good reasons for this. Much of the fresh water in the UK is under 10 feet deep, and in these sort of depths an echo sounder tends to give a rather coarse, unattractive picture when compared to its performance in deeper water.

At these shallow depths fish also become aware of the boat's presence, particularly if it is driven by a diesel or petrol engine, and will scatter before they are detected by the sounder. An electric outboard or trolling motor is useful in these circumstances.

Rivers are not good places to use fishfinders, both because of the relative shallowness of water, and the fact that the suspended silt stirred up by the water flow produces a rather 'dirty' picture.

Despite these reservations fishfinders can be very useful in certain fresh waters such as deep lakes, lochs and reservoirs. In fact depth sounders perform particularly well in clear fresh water because the signal does not suffer from the attenuation or dissipation caused by the suspended particles in the sea. So even a fairly low-power machine will give good performance in most lakes. What's more, the fish really do show up as those arches so beloved by the sales brochures.

A sounder is particularly useful on a lake or reservoir if you are new to an area, or on holiday. In this situation you are at a significant disadvantage compared to the locals, who will know the best fishing spots from many years of experience (and many days of landing no fish).

With a sounder you can survey the lake in a couple of hours, locating not only the places where the fish congregate, but also

There is a common misconception that fish can hear or feel the ultrasonic pulse emitted by the transducer. The facts are that although fish in shallow water may scatter as the boat approaches, fish in deep water will quite happily stay a few feet under the hull with a sounder running. Experts think that this is because the fish feel secure in deep water, because they have plenty of space beneath them to dive into; in shallow water, on the other hand, they have a limited escape options and are therefore less likely to risk close proximity to a potential threat.

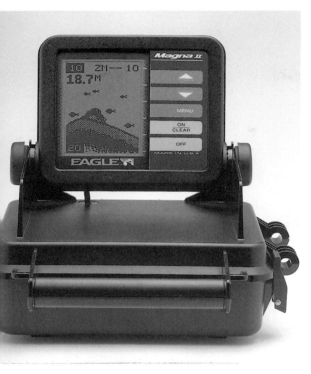

ABOVE **The Eagle Magna II portable fishfinder is mounted on a power pack containing two six-volt lantern batteries.**

LEFT **A portable transducer with a suction cup mount, ideal for use in small boats in calm water.**

Portable transducers and sounders

Many useful fishfinder accessories are available for freshwater anglers.

Several manufacturers offer a portable transducer that has a large suction pad attachment; this enables it to be stuck to the transom of a small boat just below the waterline. This option is designed for rowing boats and boats with low-power outboards, since it is not suitable for high-speed use.

Portable power packs are available for some of the lower-powered liquid crystal models. These normally accept two 6-volt lantern-type batteries and give several hours of continuous use. Rechargeable versions of these batteries are also available. The pack often folds into a handy carrying case, making it ideal for use in hire boats.

The sidescan transducer

Designed to fit at the bottom of a trolling or electric outboard motor, this works rather like a sonar by directing a beam sideways. If no trolling motor is available, it can be attached to the end of a pole and submerged in about three feet of water. Although the range of a sidescan unit is limited to about 120 feet, it is useful for scanning the area around the boat for fish,

the deep spots and holes that will give good potential. The notes you make during those two hours will be worth more than several years of fishing without a sounder.

For example, I have made several visits to Bewl Bridge Reservoir in southern England, and watched anglers fishing near the middle of the main body of water where my sounder has registered very few fish. But when I surveyed one of the arms of the reservoir, over a flooded stream and the remains of an old mill, the display showed a mass of fish echoes – yet there was not an angler in sight! Some of the anglers fishing the middle of the lake must have been fairly experienced, yet I had discovered a hotspot that none of them were aware of.

People involved in fish conservation are often concerned about the increasing use of fishfinders. They reason that if every angler on a lake had a fishfinder, there would shortly be no fish left.

Scientists in the USA have done considerable research into this, and have concluded that rod and line fishing can never clear a lake because natural regeneration restocks the water as quickly as the fish are taken out. In other words, if a significant number of large fish are removed by anglers, the greater availability of food and lack of predators will increase the number of young fish that grow to maturity.

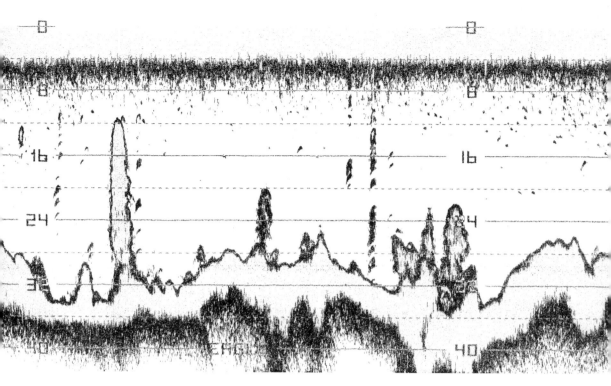

ABOVE **A paper trace recorded by an Eagle Mach 1 at Bewl Bridge Reservoir, showing fish congregating around the submerged ruins of a building and a number of tree stumps.**

both in open water and along the edges of vertical drop-offs.

Anglers should, however, be aware that the beam will be reflected back from the underside of the surface, painting an echo at the appropriate distance on the display. This can be confusing, and distinguishing fish from other echoes requires careful interpretation of the picture.

The sidescan transducer can also be used to locate carp and other species from the lake side or river bank, offering land-based anglers the benefits of an echo sounder for the first time.

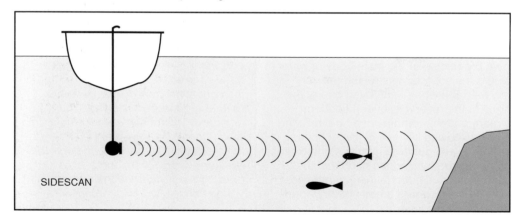

SIDESCAN

THE CHRISTMAS TREE EFFECT

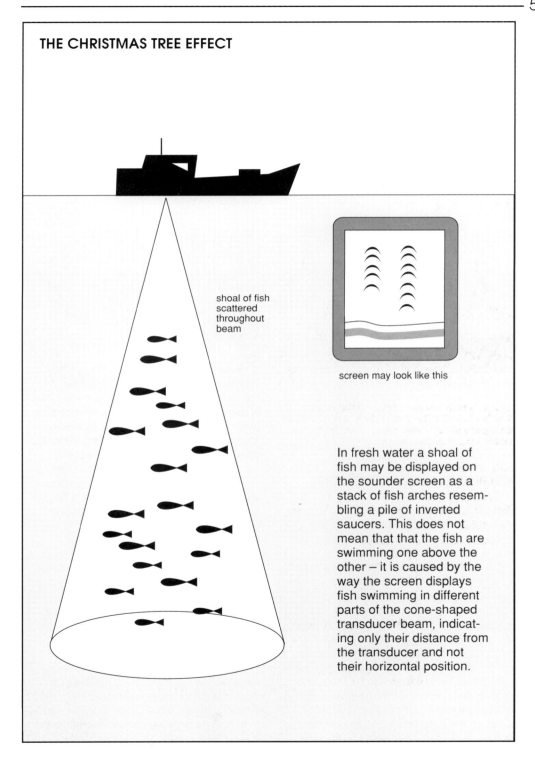

shoal of fish scattered throughout beam

screen may look like this

In fresh water a shoal of fish may be displayed on the sounder screen as a stack of fish arches resembling a pile of inverted saucers. This does not mean that that the fish are swimming one above the other – it is caused by the way the screen displays fish swimming in different parts of the cone-shaped transducer beam, indicating only their distance from the transducer and not their horizontal position.

Carp angling with a fishfinder BY ANDY LITTLE

Andy Little is one of the most respected and successful carp anglers of our time. He has caught more carp weighing over 30 pounds in the UK than anyone else. In the UK his largest carp is 41 lb 8 oz while his all-time best is a 53 lb mirror carp from Bulgaria. He has written many books on carp fishing, and has a regular weekly column in the Angler's Mail. *Andy is an active B.C.S.G. and Carp Society member, has designed many innovative items of tackle and is a consultant for both D.A.M. and Richworth Baits.*

Here is an insight into how Andy has successfully used fishfinders on many of his pioneering trips abroad.

In the USA fishfinders are widely used on lakes and rivers, but in Europe and the UK they are employed almost exclusively by sea anglers. In fact there is plenty of scope for fishfinders in freshwater, particularly on large, deep lakes, and I have found them a great help on many occasions.

FISHING SNAGGY RESERVOIRS

Many of the waters that I tackle in Europe are huge reservoirs, mostly in excess of a thousand acres and sometimes as much as five thousand acres.

The problem with many of these reservoirs is that they are just dammed-up valleys. A small river that once wound its way through vineyards and small villages has been transformed into a huge sheet of open water. When these barrages are constructed, the water quickly builds up behind, and the finished depths can sometimes be in excess of 200 feet. The underwater contours change dramatically throughout the length of the reservoir, because the original landscape remains more or less intact beneath the surface.

Trees, vineyards, fences and small buildings lie at the bottom of many of these waters.

This is where fishfinders come into their own. To find a suitable area, I will normally take to the water with a small boat and use a fishfinder as my 'eyes' on the lake bed. The model I am currently using is a Portable Compact Eagle Fish I.D. II. This has an easily-used display showing the depth and the contours of the bottom. Using three sizes of fish symbols, it also gives me a good idea of just what is inhabiting the area. These portable units are powered by two six-volt batteries which fit neatly into the carrying case. An extension lead runs down to a suction mounted transducer which is easily fixed below the waterline on the boat's hull.

A day out on the water will give me a wealth of information: exactly where the fish are concentrated, at what depth they are swimming, and probably most important of all, where the snaggy areas are located! It's no good just finding the fish, only to lose them among a forest of sunken trees.

I well remember tackling a two-thousand-acre lake. We had located a large shoal of carp, but they were in an area that was strewn with old vineyards. Further searching with the sounder revealed an open area of land adjacent to the vines which appeared to be some sort of paddock, and the depth here was comparable to that of the area where the shoal was swimming. I baited the area heavily with a big bed of maize to try to draw the fish away from the sanctuary of the sunken vines.

The plan worked perfectly – in fact within a few hours of the initial baiting I landed a 42 lb mirror carp, and went on to record a memorable catch of 20 lb and 30 lb fish. Although the carp were rolling on the surface some 100 metres to my right

over the vineyards they regularly visited my baited area, allowing me to build up a substantial catch. If I had fished just where the carp had been showing, I know I would have landed very few fish, for the majority would have been lost to the snaggy vines.

FISHING HUGE LAKES

An exploratory trip to Bulgaria confronted me with one of the largest lakes that I have ever fished. It was over 25 miles long and, in places, two miles wide. Where do you start to look for fish on such an inland sea? The size was not the only problem, for the lake itself had very few features. The depth was fairly uniform between two and three metres for over 90 per cent of the water. Part of the

ABOVE **Andy with a superb 30-pound common carp taken from a reservoir in France with the aid of a fishfinder.**

lake was commercially fished – they actually used ocean-going trawlers to net table-sized fish.

This was another occasion when I was glad that I took the fishfinder along. I borrowed a suitably sized boat with an outboard motor, and set off to explore. For over an hour, not one fish could be located, and then I stumbled across one of the largest shoals of carp that I had ever seen. I estimated it to be some 100 metres long by about 25 metres wide, but I had no idea just how many fish this shoal contained.

After some ten hours afloat with the echo sounder a pattern emerged. Vast areas of the lake were barren. When fish were located they were in their hundreds, but they were always on the move.

I quickly developed a plan of action. The first stage was to use the sounder to find a shoal of fish within easy casting distance of the bank, and determine the direction in which they were moving, and how fast. This was critical, for the aim was to ambush them *en route*. Getting well ahead of the shoal, I would lay down a big bed of bait to detain them briefly. Sometimes I would catch 20 or more like this, but sometimes only two or three before the shoal passed on. Once the action stopped I was back in the boat, sounder on, in hot pursuit of another shoal.

On that particular trip I had one of the best catches that I have ever landed in Bulgaria, including mirror carp weighing more than 50 lbs and some huge plankton-eating carp of which the best weighed some 75 lbs. Yet without the sounder it would have been like fishing for a needle in a haystack.

FISHING RIVERS

It is not only lakes that offer opportunities to use a fishfinder. Many Continental rivers also contain huge carp. On one occasion the river in question, although not very wide, was long and winding and no boats were allowed. But the water was quite deep and the bank was tree-lined with very little access. I walked many miles along the river, but there were no carp to be seen.

Happily I had my trusty sounder with me, and I was able to borrow a 15-metre roach pole from one of the local anglers. Discarding the top two sections, which were too slender, I strapped the transducer to the end of the pole. This allowed me to search from the margins to about 12 metres out from the bank. With the power pack and display unit strapped around my neck, I searched every nook and cranny for carp. Before long the sounder was

showing small groups of fish lurking in favoured spots, generally in threes and fours but sometimes up to ten at a time. I noted their positions baited accordingly and returned some hours later – after returning the pole to my new-found friend – and spent a lovely couple of days catching consistently from my newly discovered hotspots.

IT HAPPENS TO THE BEST OF US

Fishing is not always a success story, and even the most experienced can be caught out by the simplest things. On one occasion I was afloat with my latest all-singing, all-dancing echo sounder, proudly pointing out to a friend all the marvellous spots from where we were going to bag up. One of these spots was quite unbelievable. Every time we went over it the sounder registered a huge shoal of massive carp. We seemed to be set up for a record-breaking day, but we fished the area for hours and hours and had not a twitch. Nor did we see any sign of fish.

We tried again with the echo sounder, and yes, they were still there. I decided that some disturbance might stimulate them into feeding, so I made several casts through the shoal of fish with a heavy lead on the end of the line. But still we sat there. This was getting desperate.

A re-check with the sounder still showed this huge shoal of carp, and since the water was only about three metres deep my companion decided that he would go in and join them. The water was reasonably clear, and he felt that even if we couldn't catch them we could at least see them. So in he went, only to reappear a few minutes later almost hysterical with laughter. The fact was that there was not a fish in sight – only some metal pillars from a bridge that had long since been demolished. We were getting false echoes from the pillars, and these were kidding us into thinking we had found the grandaddies of all carp!

Having installed an echo sounder, you will probably want to buy an electronic navigator. This is a device which will give you, at the very least, an accurate position in latitude and longitude, and generally a lot more information as well.

Four types of electronic position fixing devices are available to small boat users.

Decca

Developed during World War 2 to assist in the D-day landings, the Decca system uses groups of land-based transmitting stations, each group consisting of a master and three slaves, to broadcast a series of signals at very low frequency. The receiver on your boat measures the difference in phasing between the master and slaves to calculate a position.

Until the early 1980s a Decca set was a heavy, bulky piece of equipment with a display that included three dials coloured red, green and purple. The set had to be

rented from the Decca company, and used in conjunction with a special chart overlaid with a lattice of numbered lines in at least two of these colours. By interpolating the numbers on the dials a position could be found on the chart.

The original Decca sets were eventually superseded by a wave of relatively low-priced models which, after some legal wrangling, were offered for sale direct to the public. The new generation of sets used microprocessor technology to convert the signals directly into a latitude and longitude position, as well as a variety of other information, and until recently these Decca units were the first choice for anyone working in northern European waters.

The system is essentially an inshore one, with a maximum range of one to two hundred miles. Most Decca sets update the position displayed every 2.5 seconds, although one or two of the low-priced sets update every 20 seconds. Accuracy varies

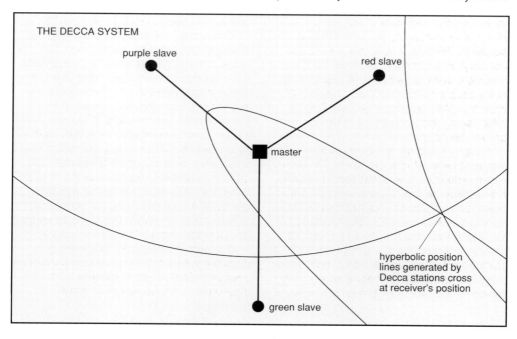

THE DECCA SYSTEM

purple slave

red slave

master

green slave

hyperbolic position lines generated by Decca stations cross at receiver's position

between night and day, summer and winter, but fortunately for pleasure users the best performance is obtained by day in the summer when accuracies of 100 yards are possible. On a winter's night, accuracies (or rather, inaccuracies) of up to two miles are not uncommon.

The main disadvantage of Decca is that it is affected by interference, both from other equipment on the boat, and externally from the atmosphere, electrical storms and other transmissions. Certain sea areas near transmitting stations and under high cliffs also suffer poor signal quality which results in position errors.

The most extensive Decca coverage is in north-western Europe, between Norway and Portugal. One or two other, relatively small, areas of the world are also covered, including Hong Kong, part of northern Australia and South Africa.

In the late 1980s a question mark hung over the future of Decca in the UK when, for a while, it was thought that the American Loran C system would supersede it. But following a statement from the Department of Transport in June 1991 it is clear that Decca will be kept running for at least another 15 years.

Loran C

This is a very similar system to Decca, except that it calculates time differences between signals rather than phasing. It does have a greater range than Decca, but it is limited in coverage to certain parts of the world such as the North American continent, the Mediterranean and the North Atlantic.

A number of American manufacturers have produced fishfinders combined with Loran C navigators. This has been frustrating for British and European users, who could not use the navigator part of the system. Many people hoped that Decca versions of these combined units would be introduced. Unfortunately this never happened since the potential world market for this conversion was relatively small, and of course GPS was just around the corner.

ABOVE **A Decca navigator, showing the distance and bearing to a preset waypoint, and the fact that the boat is 0.04 nautical miles off-track.**

Transit Satnav

Not to be confused with GPS, this was an earlier satellite navigation system introduced in 1964 – although practical, compact small-boat models were not introduced until about 1980.

The system had its shortcomings, for although each fix was accurate to 200 yards or so, the fixes were not continuous – indeed there were often gaps of an hour or more between them. The sets used a dead reckoning system to 'navigate' between fixes, so although fine for a yacht on an ocean passage, the system was not much use on fast inshore craft which need a system that updates continuously.

These three electronic navigation systems have served mariners well in different ways, in different parts of the world, over the last 40 years. Unfortunately each had at least one of the following drawbacks: either it did not give continuous updated information, it was restricted in its area of operation, or it suffered from various sources of interference. What was needed was a system without any of these limitations, and this has now been developed – GPS.

13 THE GLOBAL POSITIONING SYSTEM: GPS

Conceived in 1973, GPS is a virtually ideal electronic navigation system. The theory is essentially very simple. Any position on earth can be computed if the computer can determine the exact distance to four orbiting satellites. And if those satellites are high enough above the earth's surface, the measurements will be practically interference-free.

After some delays arising from problems with the Space Shuttle the complete system is now in operation, consisting of a constellation of 21 satellites, plus three spares, orbiting the earth twice a day at an altitude of 11,000 miles.

The key to its operation are the very precise electronic clocks found in both the satellites and the receivers. These are synchronised so that the time taken for a coded signal to reach the receiver from the satellite can be measured precisely. Knowing that the speed of the signal is constant, the distance to that satellite can then be computed. Measure the distance to three other satellites, and you can fix a position on the earth's surface.

The speed of the coded radio signal is the same as the speed of light: 186,000 miles per second – so the clocks have to be very precise indeed with an accuracy of one nanosecond. That's 0.000000001 second! This gives a potential accuracy of 10 yards.

BELOW **The constellation of GPS satellites orbiting the earth.**

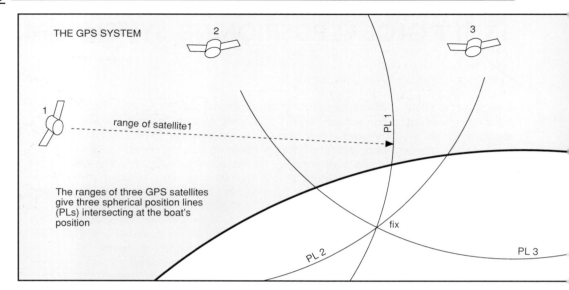

THE GPS SYSTEM

range of satellite1

PL 1

PL 2

PL 3

fix

The ranges of three GPS satellites give three spherical position lines (PLs) intersecting at the boat's position

I say potential, because GPS is a military system owned and operated by the US government. In order to protect military targets two codes are generated, the 'P' or 'Precise' code that only military sets can receive, and the 'C/A' or 'Coarse Acquisition' code for civilian receivers. The C/A code can be – and is – degraded by an operational mode called Selective Availability which can reduce the accuracy of receivers to around 50-100 metres.

In spite of these restrictions GPS is still a remarkably accurate and interference-free method of navigation – and it is available worldwide. Computer technology also means that the receivers will do very much more than simply display a basic lat/long position.

Single-channel multiplex

Information must be received from four satellites to obtain a position fix. A single-channel unit uses only one channel, and switches continually between satellites to obtain its information. Several of the less expensive sets use this system, which is adequate for slow boats. However, because such units update relatively slowly they cannot instantly reflect changes in course and speed, so they are not really suitable for fast planing craft.

Multi-channel

A multi-channel receiver can track three or more satellites simultaneously, often while a spare channel is searching for the next satellite. Not only does this give a more accurate fix, but it also shows any changes in boat speed and direction, almost immediately. Such sets are also affected less by selective availability.

A few manufacturers, notably the Lowrance/Eagle company, have recently introduced a range of models with combined GPS and fishfinder displays, and these are the type we are going to look at.

INSTALLING A GPS/FISHFINDER

Although GPS receivers are high-tech devices they are easy to install on small boats. Installation should take no more than an hour or so. So let's see how to install a typical combined unit: the Lowrance LMS 350 GPS.

The set is supplied with an owner's manual, an aerial, aerial cable, transom-mount transducer, power lead, in-line fuse, mounting bracket and knobs, aerial collar, fairing and aerial mounting adapter – although these last three items are not always needed.

1 The first stage is to find a suitable mounting position for the display. The Lowrance/Eagle models are totally waterproof, so an outside location – say behind a windscreen in a position easily viewed from the helm – is quite acceptable. Remember to allow sufficient clearance behind the display to plug in the various cables.

2 Screw or bolt the bracket to that position: if you are bolting through thin fibreglass, you may need a wooden backing piece to prevent the display wobbling at speed.

3 Next plug in the power lead and connect the cables to your 12-volt supply – either direct to the battery using the in-line fuse in the red positive lead, or via a fuse panel. The cables can be extended using similar-sized wire, but bear in mind that you will get voltage drops if the run is too long. If you are connecting direct to the battery, fit the in-line fuse as close to the power source as possible.

4 You will also notice one or two other cables extending from the power lead assembly. These are the NMEA interface cables. The white one found on all the Lowrance/Eagle models is used to transfer the GPS information to another piece of equipment such as a radar or autopilot; it is normally a straightforward run to a connection in the back of the set involved – but do check the other instrument's manual before proceeding. The green cable, found only on the later models, allows information from other equipment to be displayed on the GPS screen.

5 Next fit the transducer for the echo sounder. The set is normally supplied with a transom-mount transducer, but this can be changed by your dealer for a different type if required. The transducer simply plugs into the back of the display and the installation of the various types is covered fully in Chapter 2.

6 The small, squat aerial should ideally be mounted in an outside position with a clear view of the sky and horizon. It should not be mounted high up, or at any great distance from the display, since the

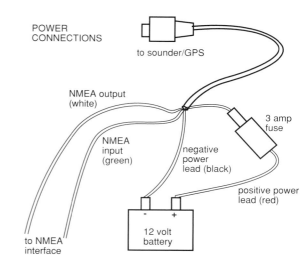

POWER CONNECTIONS

to sounder/GPS

NMEA output (white)

NMEA input (green)

negative power lead (black)

3 amp fuse

positive power lead (red)

to NMEA interface

12 volt battery

position shown on the screen is the position of the aerial. In fact, masthead mountings on yachts are discouraged because, particularly in rough water, the mast's arc of swing can show up as position changes on the display.

Two mounting positions are available. The aerial can be bolted directly onto a flat surface such as a coachroof, either by through-drilling or by using the optional clamping collar which can be used to screw the aerial down from above (although the cable hole will of course still have to be drilled).

If this is not appropriate the aerial can be screwed to the top of a standard VHF aerial bracket or extension pole via a short adaptor. A plastic fairing is supplied for this mounting option which gives the aerial a streamlined appearance; it also contains a set screw that prevents it unscrewing itself or skewing round on the pole.

Although an outside position is strongly recommended, experience has shown that signals can be received through sailcloth and thin perspex. However, the set may not register satellites near the horizon if the aerial is surrounded by too much solid material.

Unlike Decca and Loran C, GPS navigators do not require earthing.

ABOVE **A Lowrance GPS aerial attached to a VHF ratchet mount via an adaptor, and mounted on the side of an A-frame at the back of a RIB. This is an ideal position: not too high but with an almost uninterrupted 'view' of the horizon.**

THE INITIALISATION SEQUENCE

You have now fitted the power lead, transducer and aerial, plugged the cables into the back of the display and switched on. If nothing happens, re-check all the connections – particularly to the battery.

Many of the earlier sets needed to be initialised. That is, they had to be told where they were on the earth's surface, and programmed with the time, date and height above sea level. You did this only once, the very first time you switched on, unless you intended to carry the set a great distance – say several thousand miles – between uses.

The most recent models are able to initialise themselves, and simply require you to press the 'on' button after the unit has been installed. The set will then take about 15 minutes to lock onto the satel-

lites and display a position. This function is called 'Cold start' or 'Anywhere fix'.

On the earlier sets, and to speed satellite acquisition on the later models, the initialisation information is entered by the operator. One thing to note is that the instructions on the screen are annoyingly logical and cannot be ignored. You must follow the steps exactly, otherwise the information you are trying to programme will be rejected. For instance, if the time is 7.30 am, you must enter it as 073000.

The set will first ask for your position. This means that you must enter your present position on the water. But where do you find this information?

All charts have a border that shows latitude down the side and longitude across the top. By laying a straight edge first horizontally, and then vertically against your position, you can read off the latitude and longitude from this border. Alternatively, span the distance between your position and the nearest grid lines on the chart using a pair of dividers, and transfer these measurements to the border; this method gives a more accurate result.

Let's say you are launching from Swanage jetty on the south coast of England. By reference to the chart you can see that your latitude is 50 36.4" north, that is 50 degrees 36.4 minutes north of the equator, and your longitude is 1 57.2" west, that is 1 degree 57.2 minutes west of the Greenwich meridian. There are 60 minutes in a degree.

You enter this position into the receiver as follows: 50 36.400 001 57.200. Note that the minutes must be entered to three decimal places. It is not necessary to be this exact, but the spaces must be filled, so simply enter zeros. In this instance it is also important that the degrees longitude are entered using three figures, so insert two zeros before the figure one.

Before accepting this position, the unit will check whether the latitude is to be entered as north or south (that is, north or south of the equator), and whether the longitude should be east or west (east or west of the Greenwich meridian). Having

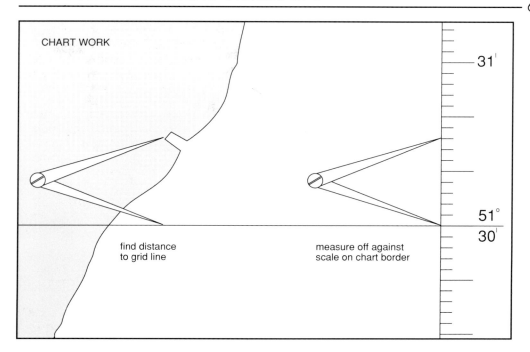

CHART WORK

31'

51°
30'

find distance
to grid line

measure off against
scale on chart border

confirmed north and west, you can then enter your position.

Don't worry about finding your exact position: anything within 200 miles is quite acceptable!

Next you enter the present time using the 24 hour clock, then the date, remembering to use the American format of month, then day, then year.

Finally you must tell the navigator how high you are above sea level. On a boat at sea this will of course simply be the height of the aerial. The set will then compute its position.

STATUS DISPLAY

When the receiver has locked onto four satellites your position will appear on the screen. On earlier sets the words 'data invalid' flash, changing after a few seconds to alternate with 'in acquisition mode'. If this does not happen after a minute or two, consult the manual.

Experience has shown that a Lowrance/Eagle GPS receiver normally takes about three minutes to obtain its very first fix when initialised by the operator. This is always confirmed by a short audible tone. On all subsequent occasions fixes are obtained in about 30 seconds, providing enough usable satellites are in view.

You can monitor the receiver's progress as it locks onto satellites by selecting the Status Display page where the satellites are listed in a table of five columns.

The first of these, headed 'PRN', is simply the satellite's reference number. Some of the numbers are above 21 because the present constellation numbers run on from a group of earlier prototypes. Next, under the heading 'TRK', which stands for track, you can see if the satellite is being searched for ('S'), or found and tracked ('T'). The column headed 'ELV' shows the elevation, that is the angle between the horizon (0°) and right overhead (90°). As a general rule the higher elevation is better; usable elevations lie between 5° and 85°. 'AZM' is the azimuth – the satellite's bearing from your position – 0° being north and

CH#	PRN	TRK	ELV	AZM	SNR
1	26	T	5°	160°	36
2	12	T	71°	40°	42
3	23	T	6°	231°	43
4	01	T	32°	307°	40
5	20	T	41°	240°	41

DOPS
H- 1.83 T- 1.55
G- 3.30 V- 2.26
P- 2.91

VISIBLE SATS
12 20 13 01
21 23 26

POSITION
N 50° 47.621'
W 1° 11.708'

SOG
0.2 KN

COG
320° MAG

DTG
1.81 NM

BRG
132° MAG

TIME/DATE
11:42:45 AM
5/10/1993

MADE IN U.S.A.

ABOVE **The status display, showing the satellite positions in the sky, reference number and fix quality (top left); the GDOP and all 'visible' satellites (top right). Beneath these are our present position, speed over ground (SOG), course over ground (COG), distance to go (DTG), bearing to the next waypoint (BRG) and the time and date.**

180° being south as on a compass rose. Finally the column headed 'SNR' shows the signal-to-noise ratio, i.e. the ratio between the clear signal and the interference and hash. The higher the number, the better; a good fix will be in the thirties and forties.

Depending on your machine, you will also see some or all of the following: 'GDOP', 'HDOP', 'VDOP' and 'TDOP'. These stand for the tongue-twisting Geometric Dilution of Precision, a combination of Horizontal Dilution of Precision, Vertical Dilution of Precision and Time Dilution of Precision.

GDOP refers to the area of uncertainty around a fixed position caused by the crossing angles between the various satellites, as seen from that position. A small angle gives scope for greater error, and just in the case of conventional position fixing, a large angle gives less error. The smaller the number, the better the crossing angles; 2.5 is excellent, 4.0 is moderate, and if the number is anything above 4.0 the position is changing erratically. Following the GDOP trend gives you

GEOMETRIC DILUTION OF PRECISION (GDOP)

we're somewhere
in this shaded area

at close angles
the area gets bigger

A large angle between satellites gives a small, square area of potential error, or low GDOP, so your actual position is close to that given by the navigator.

A small angle between the satellites gives an elongated area of potential error, or high GDOP, and your real position could be some distance from that indicated.

a better opportunity of assessing the accuracy at any particular time.

The earlier models also showed a fix reference number of between one and nine. The higher number the better the fix, although now that all the satellites are in position it rarely shows less than nine. The reference '2D' or '3D' indicates either a two- or three-dimensional fix. A three-dimensional fix simply confirms the height indicated above sea level – useful for glider and aircraft pilots, but of only passing interest to mariners.

THE NAVIGATION DISPLAY

If you switch back to one of the navigation screens, you can now read your position to three decimal places of a minute. The receiver updates itself every second, so as your boat moves through the water the position displayed will constantly be changing. Even when stationary, the decimals will probably be changing. This is called jitter, and is one of the effects of Selective Availability.

Like any electronic or radio position indicator, GPS is an aid to navigation and should not be relied upon as the only means of position fixing. The set will only operate for as long as you have a supply of electricity. A fault in the charging system or a waterlogged battery could leave you without that supply, so your boat should also be equipped with at least a compass and a chart. You should also learn how to use them by taking a course in basic navigation. This will help you shape a course using the GPS, so your money will be well spent even if your electronics perform faultlessly.

Other navigation functions

As well as your position, the navigation screens show additional information in headed boxes. Let's run through these one by one.

COG is course over the ground. If you were steering due north, unaffected by wind or tide, the course shown by your

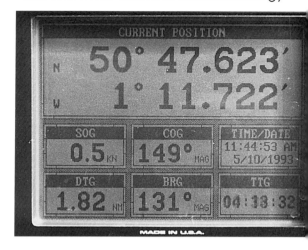

ABOVE **The navigation display, showing the current position as a lat/long figure. The screen also shows the speed over ground (SOG) as 0.5 kt, the course over ground (COG) as 149° magnetic, the time and date, the distance to go to the next waypoint (DTG) as 1.82 nautical miles, and the bearing of the waypoint (BRG) as 131° magnetic. It also gives the time to go (TTG) before we get there as 4 hours, 13 minutes and 32 seconds!**

compass would be 0° and your course over the ground would also be 0°. But if a tidal current started up, moving from west to east, your boat – although still pointing north – would be pushed maybe 10° to the east at a crabwise angle. Your compass would still show a northerly heading but your COG would be 010°.

BRG is bearing. That is, the compass bearing of a destination you have previously programmed; more about this later.

XTE is cross-track error. Imagine a straight line between your start position and the destination you have programmed; this is your track. The cross-track error is simply your distance away from that line.

DTG is the distance to go to your destination.

TTG is the time to go, assuming your present speed is maintained until you reach your destination.

TOD is simply time of day. Incidentally, the receiver's internal clock keeps running even when the set is switched off.

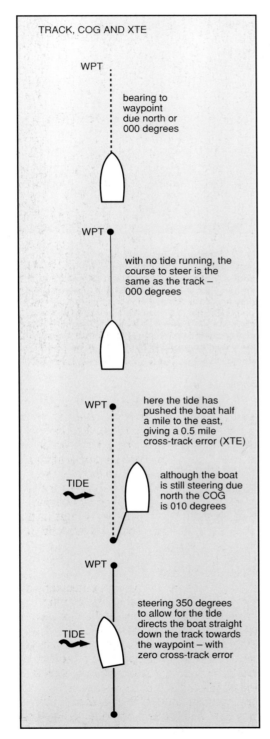

TRACK, COG AND XTE

WPT

bearing to
waypoint
due north or
000 degrees

WPT

with no tide running, the
course to steer is the
same as the track –
000 degrees

WPT

here the tide has
pushed the boat half
a mile to the east,
giving a 0.5 mile
cross-track error (XTE)

TIDE

although the boat
is still steering due
north the COG
is 010 degrees

WPT

TIDE

steering 350 degrees
to allow for the tide
directs the boat straight
down the track towards
the waypoint – with
zero cross-track error

ALT is altitude. When you are at sea this should show the height of your aerial above the water, but the effects of Selective Availability may give heights of 100-200 feet at sea level. In this respect the altitude display gives a useful indication of the degree of accuracy you can rely on.

SOG is speed over the ground, which is a particularly useful piece of information. A conventional log gives your speed through the *water*, and does not allow for the effects of wind and tide. The electronic navigator gives your actual speed over the surface of the earth.

VMG is velocity made good, and is the speed you are going *towards your destination.* This can be different to your speed over the ground if, owing to the effects of the tide, the boat is travelling at a crabwise angle.

WAYPOINT NAVIGATION

Most boat owners buy GPS, Decca and Loran C equipment for waypoint navigation. So what is a waypoint?

A waypoint is any chosen position. For a sea angler or diver it might be the position of a wreck. For a yachtsman on passage, it might be a position where the boat will be turned onto a different heading. For all mariners, a particularly useful waypoint is the position of the home port or launching slip, which can be called up at the end of the day.

A waypoint can be entered in two ways: either by the quicksave function, or by the standard method as a set of figures.

The quicksave function simply memorises the current position as a waypoint. This is particularly useful to anglers and divers, for if an interesting fishing mark or wreck appears on the fishfinder screen the position can be saved in the memory for later recall by pressing a single button.

The standard method of saving a waypoint is to enter it as a latitude/longitude position in exactly the same way as when the set is initialised, remembering that the

ABOVE **Entering a waypoint, in this case the position of a wreck. On this unit on-screen menus guide you through the procedure, and on-screen arrows indicate the buttons to press for the various functions. Here the latitude figure is about to be corrected; it is highlighted, and pressing the button indicated by the 'Change Lat' arrow will bring up a menu for making the alteration.**

minutes have three places of decimals and that the zeros, if applicable, must be inserted before the degrees longitude.

Once entered, the waypoint is automatically given the next reference number in sequence, unless instructed otherwise. Upon recall, the waypoint position is displayed with its bearing and distance from your present position – both in the waypoint lists and on the navigation steering and plotting screens.

On many sets the waypoints can be both entered and recalled by name, but some only have the facility to do this by number, in which case it is a good idea to keep a written log of the various numbers and the positions they refer too.

Routes

On a passage using a number of waypoints, it may be convenient to enter them into the navigator as a route. A route consists of several waypoints which can be pre-programmed before starting a trip; as the boat arrives at each waypoint – signalled by an alarm – the next waypoint is automatically sequenced, and its details are displayed on the screen. Routes can normally operate in reciprocal mode for a return journey.

Man overboard

Losing someone overboard, particularly at night, or in bad weather, is easier than you might think, and one of the most terrifying of all nautical emergencies. One feature of the electronic navigator is the man overboard (MOB) button which, like the waypoint quicksave function, memorises the boat's current position when it is pressed. On some of the earlier sets the waypoint quicksave mode doubled as the man overboard control.

If anyone falls from the boat someone should press the MOB button immediately. This records the current position, and also changes the screen to display it, plus some additional information.

One of these should be the *time* at which the MOB button was pressed. It is vital to realise that the MOB position indicated is not necessarily the position of the casualty. Some time may have elapsed between the actual incident and the pressing of the button, and if there is any tide running the casualty will be swept downstream from the point where he fell off the boat. If the tide is running at four knots, the victim will be 135 yards away from the position indicated after only one minute! It is therefore essential to have a record of the time when the button was pressed, taken from a wristwatch if necessary, since this will give you – and the rescue services – something to work from.

The navigator also shows the distance and bearing to the initial MOB position, and the boat's course and speed over the ground. In addition, a segment of the screen shows a plotter display that gives a bird's-eye view of the position of the boat in relation to the initial MOB position. Probably the best way to use these functions is to return to the initial MOB position as quickly as possible and then head in the same direction as the tidal stream – information which you will have to get from the chart or tidal stream atlas. And don't hesitate to get on the VHF and call for help.

Alarms

GPS navigators are equipped with at least some of the following alarms.
● Arrival alarm: This can be set to activate when the boat arrives at a specific distance from the waypoint.
● Off-course alarm: This will alert the operator when the boat drifts more than a set distance off track.
● Anchor alarm: An electronic circle is set around the boat at a chosen distance. If the boat moves out of that circle, the alarm activates.

THE PLOTTER

The plotter display is of particular interest to divers and anglers. There are two types of GPS plotter on the market. The chart plotter looks like a small television set and shows the boat's position as a cross hair superimposed on a picture of a chart. The chartless track plotter, which is the type used in the combined GPS/fishfinders, gives a bird's-eye view of your track from a start position at the centre, on an otherwise blank screen bordered by the four compass points.

Although the chart plotter may appear to give a more useful presentation, the chart information is held on rather expensive cartridges that each cover only a limited sea area. Furthermore the sets are not at all waterproof, and therefore not suitable for the open or semi-open boats normally used for fishing or diving.

The LCD chartless plotter has limited value for navigation, but it can be very helpful when you are trying to locate a wreck, since you can see at a glance the search pattern you have already completed, and make instant adjustments for the effects of wind and tide. On some models the screen can be split to display both the plotter and echo sounder pictures together, so that the sea bed profile can also be monitored during the search. To be truly useful for this work, however, the plotter should have a minimum range of a quarter mile or less.

The plotter can also be used to give a visual display of track as a straight line between a start position and a waypoint. As the boat moves towards the waypoint, its actual course is plotted, enabling you to identify any cross-track error immediately.

The latest models offer a more sophisticated display that allows you to mark the positions of say, wrecks, special fishing spots, or danger areas, with up to 500 different markers or icons. Furthermore, waypoints can be downloaded onto the plotter display and identified by small flags showing their reference numbers.

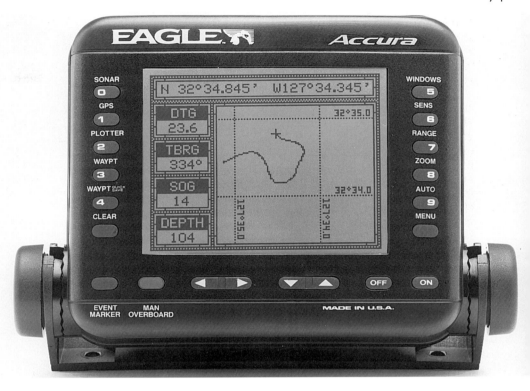

ABOVE **The plotter screen on an Eagle Accura combined GPS and echo sounder. The current position is shown by the small cross, and by the boxed information at the side. The plotter image can also be presented on a split screen or window display alongside the sounder image, enabling you to monitor both at once.**

A grid can also be superimposed on the screen which shows the position of a line of latitude and a line of longitude. The crossing point of these two lines can be moved around the display as a cursor, and placed over an icon or point of special interest to show its exact position. Then, by pressing a 'go to' button, the position can be saved as a temporary waypoint, showing navigation and steering data to that position. The cursor can also be used to place icons anywhere on the screen, to mark off danger areas, for instance.

RIGHT **A window display showing, clockwise from top left, the depth, a sounder display, a compass heading and, at bottom left, the plotter.**

Finally the screens of the latest models can be customised to show combinations of the plotter, steering and maybe echo sounder displays at the same time. These are known as window displays, and can be a real help when searching for, say, a wreck: all the relevant search information is shown on the screen at the same time, so there is no need to constantly switch from one display to the other.

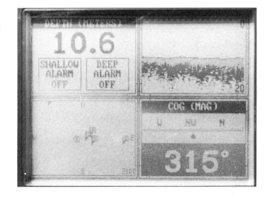

Steer to screen

This is perhaps the most visually impressive of the displays. It shows the boat as a marker, either a small circle or an arrow, and the waypoint as a larger circle, box or cross superimposed on a three-dimensional picture that resembles an airport runway. Instead of watching a compass bearing, you simply steer the boat marker down the runway until it is positioned over the shape representing the waypoint. The track is shown as a straight line down the centre of the screen, and the course steered as a line extending from behind the boat marker. The arrow representing the boat always indicates the present course over the ground.

BELOW **The steer to screen display. The waypoint is at the intersection of the four chequered quadrants of the 'runway', and the current position and orientation of the boat is indicated by the small black arrow. In this case the boat has been searching the area near the waypoint for promising contacts on the sounder, and is currently heading in the wrong direction!**

To the left and the right of the runway are lines showing the alarmed off-track limits. If the boat marker touches one of these lines, the off-track alarm sounds. This can greatly assist navigation down a narrow channel in poor visibility.

UNITS OF MEASUREMENT

GPS receivers can be programmed to show speed in miles per hour, kilometres per hour, or knots; and distance in statute miles, kilometres or nautical miles.

It is worth noting that the Lowrance and Eagle models are programmed to show speed and distance in miles per hour and statute miles after initialisation. This is because many of the sets in the USA are used on inland waterways. These default settings can however be changed to nautical miles and knots by following the on-screen menu instructions. Once this has been done the new settings are retained by the memory.

Magnetic and true

Similarly, these sets are programmed to show directions either as magnetic bearings or true bearings. Once again, they are initially set to show magnetic and have to be re-programmed to show true.

The diagram shows a sphere representing the earth's surface. At the top is the north pole, which is always at true north from any other position on earth. But the magnetic pole – which is what a compass points to – is some distance away. So from most places on earth the bearings to the true pole and the magnetic pole will be different, and that angle of difference is called the variation.

Charts are always aligned to true north, so knowing the variation is very important when taking position fixes from the land by magnetic compass. The amount of variation changes, both at different positions on the earth's surface and from year to year. However, all these changes have been pre-programmed into the combined fishfinder/GPS sets.

HORIZONTAL DATUM
The horizontal reference datum of this chart is North American Datum of 1983 (NAD 83), which for charting purposes is considered equivalent to the World Geodetic System 1984 (WGS 84). Geographic positions referred to the North American Datum of 1927 must be corrected an average of 0.413" northward and 1.920" eastward to agree with this chart.

ABOVE **The note in the margin of this American chart specifies the datum used and any correction that may be necessary. In practice, as a GPS user you simply select the appropriate datum from the list offered by your machine.**

Datum

All navigators are programmed with one or a number of chart datums, which are the results of geographical surveys.

Latitude and longitude are defined in terms of angles measured at the centre of the earth, but no-one knows exactly where that centre is. It seems to vary depending on where you are and how you measure it. As a result, different countries have adopted different centres. This in turn means that their grids of latitude and longitude – called horizontal datums – don't quite match up. In the days before satellite navigation this didn't matter very much, but worldwide navigation systems need a standard worldwide system of longitude and latitude.

The first system, called the World Geodetic System (WGS) was introduced in 1960. This has been refined and developed into WGS 84, which is the datum used in many GPS navigators. There are others, however, and some sets allow you to choose from a datum list.

Position correction

Since the earth is not a perfect sphere, GPS receivers suffer small errors in accuracy on different parts of its surface. Most machines therefore allow you to make adjustments for these errors.

The error can be found in two ways. If the boat is moored at a charted position, such as at the end of a jetty marked on a chart, the difference between that position on the chart and the position shown on

MAGNETIC VARIATION

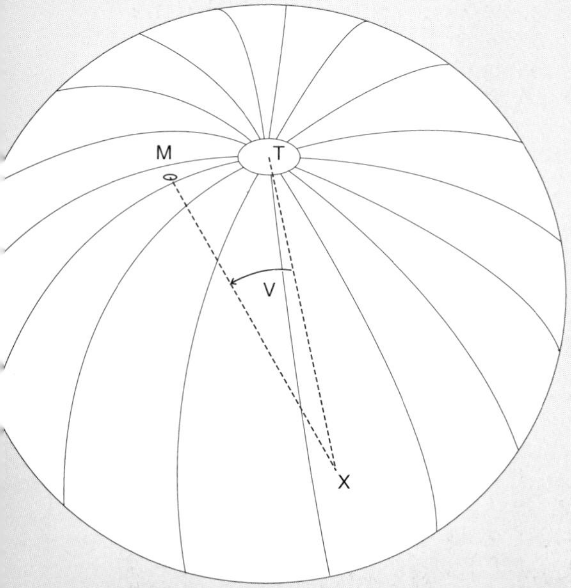

For a boat at position X the angle V is the variation between true north (T) and magnetic north (M).

the navigator can be entered as an offset. Thereafter, all positions will be offset to relate to the position of the jetty on the chart. An offset can also be found on the latest copies of Admiralty charts.

It should be stressed that these offsets are both small and localised, and you will probably never need to worry about them.

NMEA INTERFACE

In the late 1970s marine electronics had advanced to the state where different pieces of equipment could communicate or interface with each other. For example, compass information could be passed down a wire to an autopilot to give it a course to steer. To the frustration of the user, however, every manufacturer used a different interface code, so although products from the same manufacturer could interface, those from different manufacturers could not.

In 1980 a number of American marine electronics manufacturers held a conference and a standard data code was agreed known as NMEA 0180 (National Marine Electronics Association 1980). This was amended in 1982 to NMEA 0182 and again in 1983 to NMEA 0183. This standard is now used by all marine electronic manufacturers worldwide, and any of the above interfaces are available on

the GPS/fishfinders now available.

Incidentally, it may be of interest to specialist users to know that it is possible to interface a paper recording echo sounder, the Lowrance X-16, to a GPS navigator, the Lowrance Global Nav Mk1.

DIFFERENTIAL GPS (DGPS)

Devise an obstacle, and someone will always think of a way around it. So it is with Selective Availability which, as we have seen, is applied by the US Defence Department to GPS signals to deliberately reduce the accuracy of non-military (or rather, non-US military) receivers.

The differential system is operated from a network of ground stations, the positions of which have been very precisely surveyed. These ground stations calculate the position inaccuracies of the incoming GPS signals, and then transmit corrections via a radio beacon to decoders attached to GPS receivers. The effect is to increase GPS accuracy to between five and ten metres.

Currently these decoders have to be rented from the companies operating the differential system. they are not cheap, and represent a significant investment for the sports user, but it is anticipated that some countries will offer a freely available service in the future.

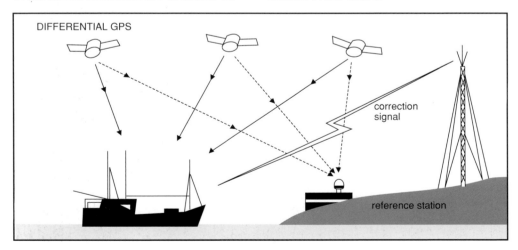

DIFFERENTIAL GPS

correction signal

reference station

14 WRECK FINDING – THE TRIP ·················

Why wrecks? Wrecks attract fish because they provide a wealth of food and because they offer a place of refuge from predators. The small fish attract big fish, and the big fish attract anglers.

The best wrecks to fish are the ones that lie at depths of 180 feet or more, and have landed on the bottom the right way up so that the superstructure is available for colonisation by weed and the microscopic creatures that form the initial stages of the food chain.

The depth of 180 feet is important, since research has shown that wrecks in water shallower than this appear to support less fish, in more transient populations. Wrecks in deeper water are colonised by larger, more stable fish populations. Moreover, shallow-water wrecks are normally closer to land; as a conse-

quence their positions are better known so they are more often fished, reducing stocks still further.

So how do you find where these productive deep-water wrecks are? Charter skippers, of course, know their positions through years of experience, but for obvious reasons they tend to keep them a closely guarded secret. You could follow a charter skipper and see where he goes, but a more sensible alternative is to put in some research.

A lot of useful information can be gleaned from the divers' guides that cover specific coastal areas. Not only are the positions and depths of the wrecks given, but also many additional background details such as the name of the vessel, how she is lying on the bottom, how she sank, and the size and height of the superstructure. This is priceless information from people who have actually been down there to have a look.

BELOW **How a wreck may be pictured on a sounder display.**

Northumberland, to Rouen with a cargo of 1,300 tons of coal. The crew was saved. Today, the *Atlas* stands upright on the seabed in 41m. It is easy to see where the torpedo struck – there is a large hole in the starboard side amidships. She lies East-West with her bows to the East. Her decks and some of her superstructure are still intact, though there is some more wreckage on the seabed on her starboard side. She stands 8m proud at 50 34 35; 00 32 52.

114 Vesuvio. At 50 35 33; 00 30 28. Sunk on April 6, 1916, this 1,391-ton British steamer was carrying a general cargo from Sicily to London when she struck a mine laid by a German submarine 6 miles East of the Owers lightship. Seven men died, including the ship's master. She now lies close to the South of a big rock reef, and rises some 5m high in 42m of water. The reef appears slightly higher than the ship which lies on her port side and is broken and silted. She lies East-West, with her bows to the East.

The latest diving information suggests that she is broken in three places on a gravel seabed, and that her propeller has been salvaged.

115 Candia. An armed British merchant steamer of 6,482 tons carrying a general cargo including lead and zinc, she was torpedoed 8 miles South of the Owers Light Vessel on July 27, 1917, while on her way back to London from Sydney, Australia. One crew member was killed. Built in 1896 as a twin-screw vessel 450ft long, it was the measurement of the overlapping arcs of those twin screws which were to give salvage divers in 1952 a positive identification of her. Those same divers salvaged 1025 tons of lead and 1,000 tons of zinc from her forward holds.

Today she is still reasonably intact in an area of great sand dunes in 45m at 50 34 18; 00 30 41. She stands 18m proud, and lies North to South.

116 Wreck, name unknown. At 50 34 04; 00 39 06, this is a small barge, 40ft long, lying on a great bank of sand and shingle in 24m. A tricky dive as the bank suddenly sweeps down to 38m just off the wreck.

ABOVE **The information on the wreck of the *Candia* published in the divers' guide *Dive Sussex* – priceless information from people who have actually been down there.**

In addition, there are two sources of chart information. In the UK the Sea Fish Industry Authority (SFIA) publishes the Kingfisher wreck charts, which have been compiled from information sent in from commercial fishermen who have snagged their trawls or lost gear on obstructions on the sea bed, and have noted these positions for future reference. It is of course these very obstructions, many of which are wrecks, that are sought after by sea anglers and divers. All the Kingfisher charts are overlaid with Decca lattice, and all positions given as Decca co-ordinates. Some of these charts now include latitude and longitude positions as well as brief information about the nature of the various obstructions.

These positions have all been fixed by Decca, and are of course subject to all the errors linked with that navigation system. Location of these wrecks with GPS will therefore be more difficult initially.

Admiralty charts also give positions of wrecks, although unless these are in shallow water and represent a hazard to shipping their accuracy may be suspect.

More detailed information on wrecks in UK waters can be obtained from the staff of the Wrecks Section of the Ministry of Defence Hydrographic Office, who can search their records and supply, for instance, specific details of a named wreck, information about all wrecks in a

RIGHT **A section of Kingfisher chart KW 150B. The position of the *Candia* is shown as number 62. Note that on all charts the depths are related to the Chart Datum or Lowest Astronomical Tide: the lowest tide that might possible occur. Normally there is a lot more water at any charted position, particularly at high tide.**

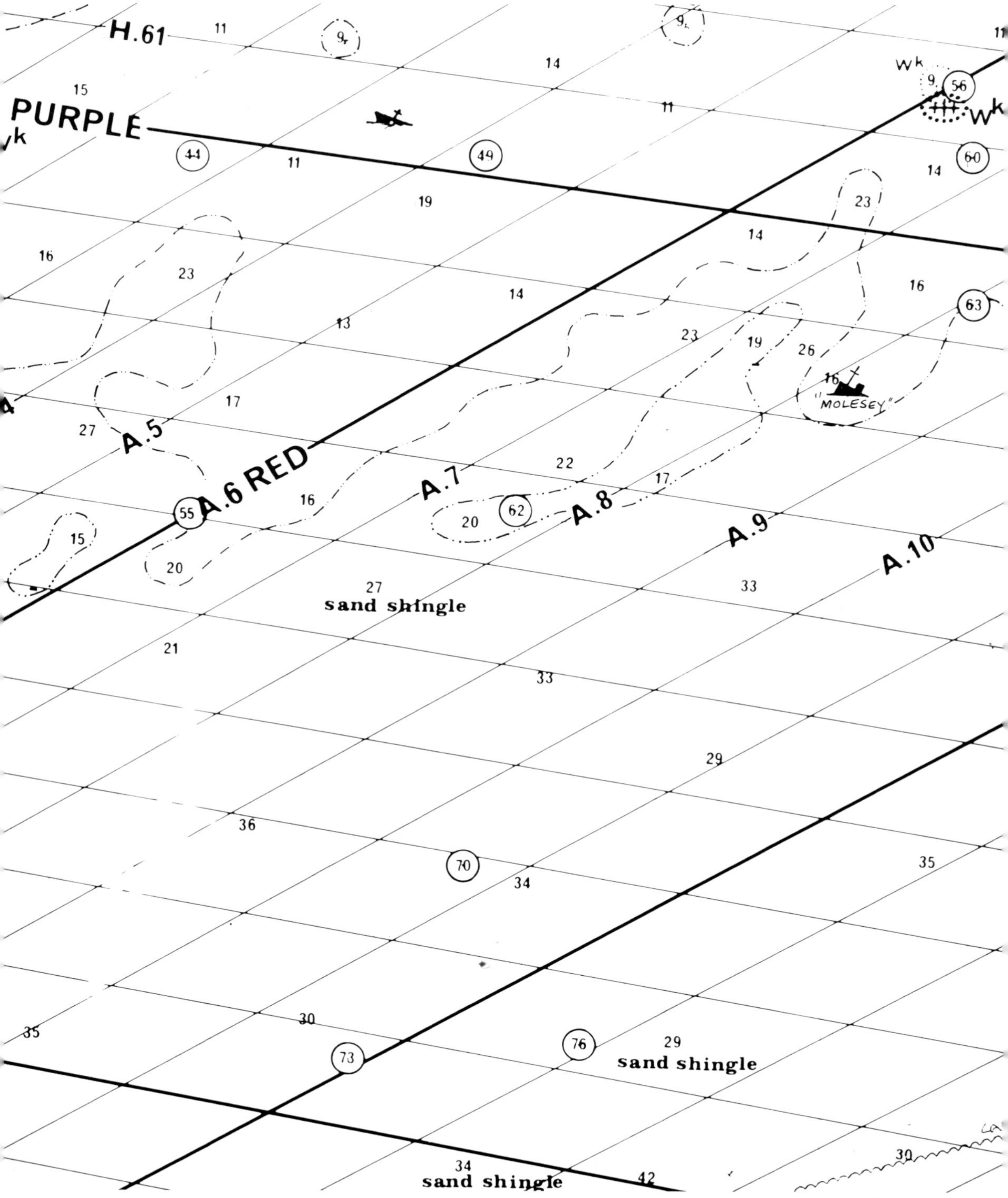
H.61
PURPLE
A.5
A.6 RED
A.7
A.8
A.9
A.10
"MOLESEY"
Wk
sand shingle
sand shingle
sand shingle
44
49
55
56
60
62
63
70
73
76

```
WRECK NUMBER:-            012301693

LATITUDE:-               51 04 20.0 N   LONGITUDE:- 001 29 27.0 E
QUALITY OF FIX:-         EDM
HORIZONTAL DATUM:-       OGB

NAME:-                   SABAC [PROBABLY]
NATIONALITY:-            YUGOSLAV
TYPE:-                   SS
TONNAGE:-                   2,811   G
DIMENSIONS:-            LENGTH:- 342 FT.   BEAM:- 46 FT.   DRAUGHT:- 20 FT.
CARGO:-                 BAUXITE
DATE SUNK:-             07 01 1962

CHART SYMBOL:-          SW       37.0 MTRS.  SW       20 FTHMS.   FT.
CHARTS(NAVIGATIONAL):-  323.1892.1610.2449.2451.1406
GEN. DEPTH:-             52 MTRS.
ORIENTATION:-           122/302
VERTICAL DATUM:-        LAT
```

CIRCUMSTANCES OF LOSS:-

VESSEL, BUILT 1922, SANK FOLLOWING COLLISION WITH BRITISH MV 'DORINGTON CASTLE' IN DENSE
FOG. OWNED AT TIME OF LOSS BY YUGOSLAV GOVERNMENT [KVARNERSKA PLOVIDBA]. VESSEL WAS
EN-ROUTE PLOCE TO ROTTERDAM. (DICTIONARY OF DISASTERS)

SURVEYING DETAILS:-

SANK 6M SE OF DOVER. (DICTIONARY OF DISASTERS)

H2088/71 15.1.71 UNKNOWN WK FOUND DURING SEARCH FOR WKS OF 'TEXACO CARRIBEAN'
& 'BRANDENBURG'. (MOD 131730Z JAN)

H2088/71 22.4.71 LARGE WK IN 510418N, 012922E. FIXED BY HSA & DECCA [ENG] RED E 6.28, GREEN
H 35.75 [U]. CLEAR AT 75FT BY OROPESA. LEAST E/S DEPTH 131 IN GEN DEPTH 160FT.
(KEDLESTONE/BEAGLE, 19.1.71)

H4988/71 4.1.72 EXAM'D IN 510414N, 012916E [EUR]. HF: PATT I [THORPENESS] 1312.13, PATT II
[S FORELAND] 2154.73. DECCA RED E 6.2. GREEN H 35.77. CLEAR AT 37. FOUL AT 37.2MTRS.
LEAST E/S DEPTH 37.5 IN 51MTRS [LAT]. LIES 123/303DEG, APPARENTLY IN ONE PIECE. LENGTH
ABT 275FT. (FAWN. H525 NO.52/71) ALMOST CERTAINLY THE SABAC DESPITE REPORTED LENGTH.

H4199/78 14.8.78 EXAM'D 30.10.77 IN 510419N, 012928E USING 2 RANGE TRISPONDER. NG CO-ORDS
644535E. 136152N. DECCA [ENG] RED E 6.17. GREEN H 35.79. EXTREMELY 'HIGH' WK. CLOSE
SOUNDED. LEAST E/S DEPTH 38 IN GEN DEPTH 54MTRS. NO SCOUR. LARGE MAST SHOWN ON DCS3
TRACE - OVERALL HT 29.3MTRS. LENGTH 120MTRS. LIES 120/300DEG. (BULLDOG. HI 35/77)

H2330/84 4.3.86 EXAM'D ON 9.12.86 IN 510420N, 012927E. NG 644507E, 136181N USING TRISPONDER
RANGES. DECCA [ENG] RED E 6.19. GREEN H 35.80. LEAST E/S DEPTH 36.9 IN GEN DEPTH 51.5
MTRS. NO SCOUR. HYDROSEARCH SHADOW HT 18.2MTRS ON HIGH POINT A THIRD WAY FROM W END.
LYING 122/302DEG WITH BOW W. 110MTRS LONG. BEAM 16MTRS. NO SIGN OF 29.3MTR HIGH POINT
REPORTED IN 1977 & WHICH IS CONSIDERED DISPROVED. RECOMMEND CHART AS SW 33.3MTRS.
(BULLDOG. HI 240B) NCA - DESPITE THIS REPORT - AWAIT WIRE-SWEEP.

H3947/88 25.5.89 EXAM'D 13.4.89 IN 510419N, 012928E USING TRISPONDER [U] & MAIN CHAIN DECCA
RED E 6.14. GREEN H 35.80. DRIFT SWEPT CLEAR AT 37.3. FOUL AT 38.9MTRS. LEAST E/S DEPTH
38.4 IN GEN DEPTH 52MTRS. NO SCOUR. HYDROSEARCH HT 13MTRS, LENGTH 102MTRS.
APPARENTLY UPRIGHT WITH SUPER STRUCTURE & FUNNEL AMIDSHIPS. WITH MAST FORE & AFT.
(ROEBUCK, HI 469)

chosen area, or even information about wrecks at certain depths in a chosen area.

An example of this information is shown opposite. It concerns the wreck of the *Sabac* lying off the south-east coast of England. Notice that its orientation on the sea bed is given. This is important, since a wreck that is lying beam-on to the tide is much easier to both locate and fish than a wreck that is lying end-on to the flow. Unfortunately most wrecks tend to end up lying along the direction of the current as they sink to the bottom. The *Sabac*, however, is shown as lying roughly northwest-southeast, and since the tide ebbs and flows more or less northeast-southwest at this position the wreck should be relatively easy to find with a sounder by doing a series of drifts in the area.

Divers

The versatility of the better LCGs and combined GPS models can be exploited to the full by divers wishing to pinpoint the

exact position of a wreck. This ability is particularly important at the diving limits of 45-50 metres, because with only a few minutes' working time available a diver needs to drop straight onto the wreck from the boat.

A sounder with a wide-beam transducer, such as the 60-degree model from the Lowrance company, is particularly useful on these occasions since it covers a large area of the sea bed. Once the wreck has been located, a narrow eight-degree beam should be used since it enables the boat to be manoeuvred directly over the wreck. A GPS plotter is also invaluable since it enables the area to be searched easily even when a tide is running. Any small deviation away from the search line shows up instantly on the screen.

An ideal sounder for wreck work should also have a good zoom facility and split screen capability. Sometimes a wreck has broken up, and zooming in on an area of the sea bed will help you spot small wreck fragments. Once located, a fragment can often be used as the start position, on a plotter, for a box or spiral search for the main body of the wreck.

BELOW **A totally waterproof LCG unit combining sounder, GPS and plotter functions is the ideal tool for wreck finding.**

A few top-range sets like the Eagle Z9500 and Accura, and the Lowrance LMS 300 and 350, have a dual-frequency capability enabling both 192 kHz and 50 kHz transducers to be used at the same time, presenting two pictures on a split screen. With this facility you can use a 50 kHz transducer with a 45-degree beam and a 192 kHz transducer with a narrow eight-degree beam to both locate and pinpoint a wreck from an uninterrupted display. This is one of the few occasions when a low-frequency transducer is useful to the sports user in shallow water.

So how do you reach the wreck from the mooring or launching point? In this case we will assume that you are hoping to locate the wreck of the *Candia,* which is lying some 14 nautical miles offshore almost due south of Littlehampton on the south coast of England (see the wreck information on page 76). The wreck chart (see page 77) gives plenty of information about the sea bed and the obstructions on it, but it is not very good for navigational purposes. In fact, a warning to this effect is printed on the chart. Even though you have a GPS navigator, with all the latest features, you must remember that it is still only an aid to navigation, and should your electrics fail, for any reason, it is important that you have a good navigational chart and a compass so you can get home safely.

There are a number of such charts on the market, suitable for small boats. Admiralty chart number 1652 (small craft edition) covering the area between Selsey Bill and Beachy Head will do very nicely.

This chart shows a large number of wrecks south of Littlehampton, including one at 50.34.60 N, 000.30.65 W. However, the positions given on the Kingfisher wreck chart, in the dive book and on the Admiralty chart are all slightly different, and some searching will almost certainly be required before the wreck can be located on the sounder.

A further complication is that the latitude/longitude positions given in the dive books, and on some of the wreck charts

are in degrees, minutes and seconds. In order to enter these positions into the navigator, the seconds must be converted into decimals of a minute; you do this by dividing the seconds by 3, multiplying by 5, then moving the decimal point two places to the right. So 30 seconds, for instance becomes 0.5 minutes:

$$30 \div 3 = 10$$
$$10 \times 5 = 50$$
50 (move decimal point) = 0.50

First you must mark the position of the wreck of the *Candia* on the chart as 'C', then put another mark 'B' about a mile to the south of Littlehampton harbour. Join the two with a line; this is called the track, and is the course you will be trying to follow. You want to go about a mile out of Littlehampton before turning to avoid any breakwaters or shallow areas.

You can now enter these positions into the navigator as waypoints. Waypoint 1 is the entrance of the River Arun, shown as 'A', and should be entered as 50.48.01 N, 000.32.45 W.

Waypoint 2 is position 'B', where you are going to alter course to get on track for the wreck site; this is entered as 50.47.00 N, 000.32.00 W.

Waypoint 3 is position 'C', the wreck of the *Candia.* For this position you have the choice of three slightly different sets of latitude/longitude coordinates, as follows:
● Kingfisher wreck chart KW 150 B (after conversion of seconds): 50.34.600 N, 000.30.683 W.
● *Dive Sussex* (after conversion of seconds): 50.34.300 N, 000.30.683 W.
● Admiralty chart 1652: 50.34.600 N, 000.30.650 W.

Since two of the latitudes and two of the longitudes are identical, it would seem reasonable to use the following position: 50.34.600 N, 000.30.683 W. You can enter this as the third waypoint.

RIGHT **A section of Admiralty chart number 1652, showing the trip start point at Littlehampton, the nominal position of the wreck of the *Candia*, the intended track and the waypoints that have been keyed into the GPS navigator.**

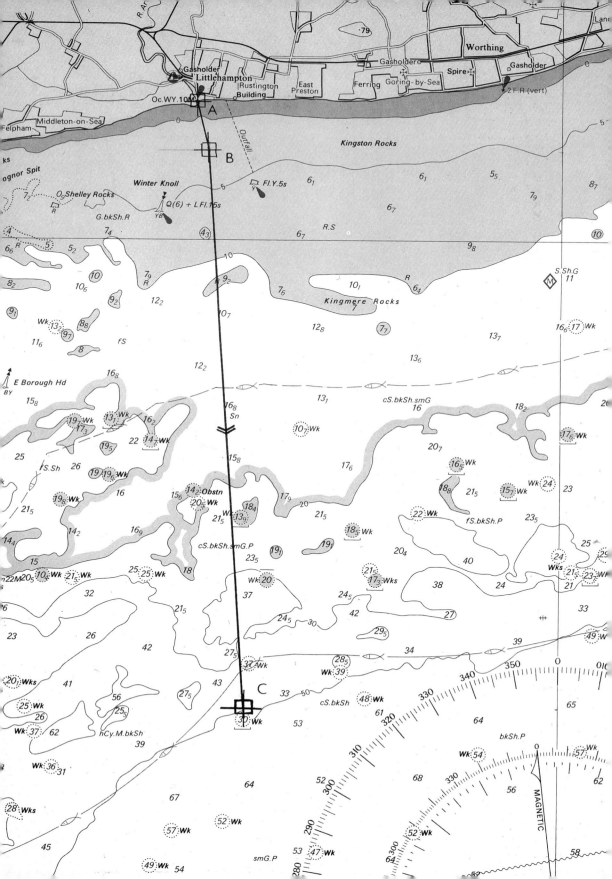

ABOVE **It's easier to enter the waypoints into the GPS while you are still on dry land. Remember to double-check all lat/long figures, and make sure you enter them in the correct format.**

Having entered the waypoints you can set the arrival alarm to, say, 0.1 mile so that you know when you are getting close to the waypoint. Don't forget that all these sets have an internal memory, so the unit can be programmed at home by simply connecting it to a 12-volt battery.

You will be steering a course of 162° (true) from the harbour entrance to Waypoint 2, and then 176° from Waypoint

BELOW **And we're off!**

2 to the position of the *Candia* at Waypoint 3. The navigator will, of course, display this information, but it is a good idea to have an idea of the various courses in case anything goes wrong with the electronics. It is also important (and interesting) to plot the boat's position on the chart as the trip progresses.

During the first part of the trip, between Waypoints 1 and 2, you will be navigating down a marked channel, taking care to avoid other craft. These waypoints are really to help on the return trip, and will be particularly useful in darkness or bad visibility. It is only when you reach position 'B' and call up Waypoint 3 that the navigator really comes into its own. It will immediately show the *Candia* as lying at a distance of 12.45 nautical miles on a bearing of 176°. Accordingly you can turn the boat onto this bearing, switch to the steer-to-screen display and watch the boat marker move down the track to the *Candia*.

After a few minutes the boat marker will start to drift to one side as the tide pushes you off-track. You must therefore adjust the boat's heading slightly to bring the marker back onto the centreline of the display – but only gradually since over-reaction will simply send the boat too far the other way. If the navigator is interfaced with an autopilot the boat will steer itself, although you must obviously keep a constant look-out for other vessels.

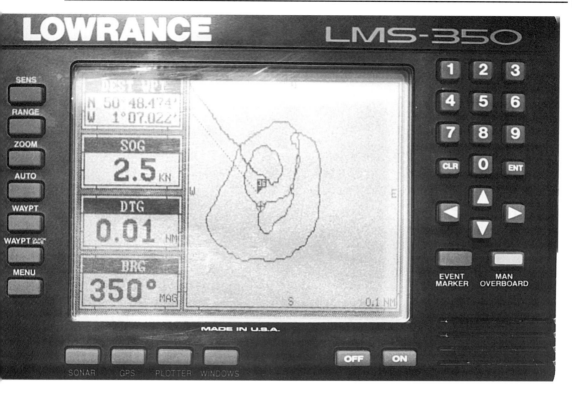

At the end of this leg you arrive at Waypoint 3: the nominal site of the wreck. If you are lucky you may locate the wreck immediately, but the chances are that you will have to start a methodical search.

Switching over to the plotter – or on the combined sets, the plotter/sounder screen

ABOVE **The plotter screen is excellent for wreck-finding. Here it shows the boat approaching Waypoint 36 (the nominal position of a wreck) and carrying out a roughly spiral search pattern. The current position is shown by the small cross, and by the information at the side. The plotter image can also be presented alongside the sounder image, so you can monitor both at once.**

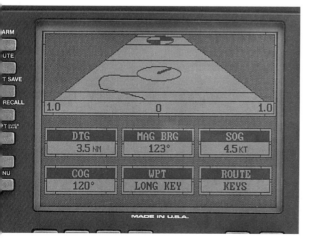

– gives a birds-eye view of the surrounding area. The radius covered by the plotter must be as small as possible to give the detail needed for the search – say one-twentieth of a mile. You then move up-tide a little before letting the boat drift back, watching the screen all the time to make small adjustments if the plotter shows that you are overlapping your previous run.

You may have to make several of these runs before the sounder shows a sudden deepening of the sea bed caused by the scouring effect of the tide around an

LEFT **Using the steer-to-screen display on a Lowrance Global Nav II.**

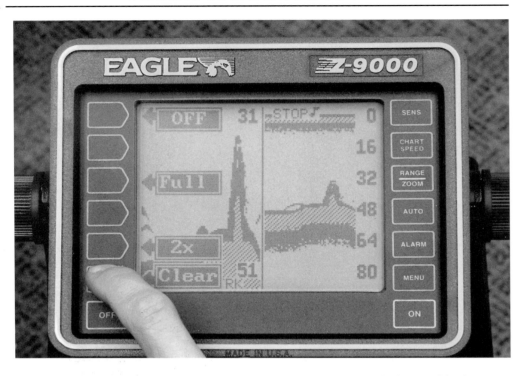

ABOVE **A wreck showing on the split-screen display of an Eagle Z-9000, in both zoom and surface-to-sea-bed mode.**

obstruction. Then it's there – the wreck, showing as a large lump on the echo sounder display.

At this point, it is a good idea to re-start the plot in the knowledge that at least part of the wreck is now at its centre. So if the wreck is being drifted for cod, for instance, you will spot any offset caused by the tide immediately and adjust the boat's position accordingly. Alternatively if you are fishing for conger you can motor up-tide again, drop the anchor and ease the boat back over the wreck.

When the boat is right over the wreck, it is a worth noting the exact position shown on the display, since this is likely to differ slightly from the position marked on your chart(s). You could also re-enter the position into the GPS set, since this will make locating the wreck much easier next time. Eventually you should be able to build up a library of very precise wreck positions

which will save much time and fuel on subsequent visits.

After the day's fishing, you need to think of the homeward journey. First, you call up Waypoint 2 on the navigator, which will take you to position 'B', one mile south of Littlehampton harbour entrance. When you reach this point you can select Waypoint 1, which was the position at the harbour entrance. In good or moderate visibility the position of the entrance only a mile away will be obvious, but if the visibility or light has failed you will find the harbour waypoint invaluable. In such conditions you must obviously take great care to avoid collision with other craft – particularly in a busy stretch of water such as the approaches to a harbour. You will also need to keep a good look-out for navigation marks and the two piers that mark the entrance to the River Arun.

Once you are back alongside, you can remove the receiver from the boat, secure in the knowledge that all the positions used on the trip have been retained in the memory for future reference.

Boat angling with a fishfinder BY STEVE MILLS

Steve Mills is a highly successful sea angler, and holds the British record for a thresher shark at 323 lb. A member of the English team that won the world championship in 1991, he is an NFSA Advanced Sea Angling Instructor and has been a regular contributor to the angling press for over 10 years. Here he describes some of the techniques he uses when boat angling with a fishfinder.

Sea fish generally favour areas where there is variation in depth, and are particularly attracted to naturally occurring features such as sand and shingle banks, channels, gulleys and reefs. Similarly an artificial feature such as a wreck will attract a great quantity and variety of fish.

The fishfinder is the boat angler's key to pinpointing these important submarine features – and locating the fish that congregate around them.

ANGLING AT ANCHOR

One of the basic principles behind anchoring is to maintain the boat 'on station' precisely over a specific mark that is known – or at least expected – to yield a quantity of fish. You may have chosen the mark from previous experience, or from information gleaned from other anglers or from chart data. You can use various navigation techniques, including electronic equipment such as GPS, to place a boat very close to such a mark, but 'very close' is generally not close enough. Your lines must be presented directly to those fish, for a few metres one way or the other can make all the difference between success and failure. In the past such precise positioning was a matter of guesswork, but the fishfinder has changed all that.

As you arrive in the vicinity of your chosen mark, slow the boat to around three or four knots. The slower the boatspeed, the greater the clarity and accuracy of information from the fishfinder.

You should now be monitoring three important parameters: the sea bed composition, the depth and the fish.

The sea bed composition is indicated by the strength of signal returned by the fishfinder. You may be looking for rough ground (rock) if species like conger, pollack, or wrasse are your target. Alternatively, you may be looking for a softer, sandy bottom if you are after fish like whiting, rays and flatfish. It is also worth making a thorough search or scan of the area to get an accurate impression of the sea bed surrounding the mark.

The actual depth is usually of less importance than the depth of your position in relation to the surrounding area. For example, your angling experience might

BELOW **Steve with a fine cod taken from a wreck site off the Isle of Wight in southern England.**

determine whether you need to fish on top of a bank, on the edge or at the base.

The fishfinder provides an alternative to experience because it can directly detect where certain fish are. Shoaling species such as members of the cod family often show clearly close to the bottom.

Once you have located the exact mark – the bank, reef or channel – you should slowly motor uptide, drop the anchor and drift back, paying out the anchor cable until the boat lies precisely over the mark.

Anchoring on an offshore sandbank which lies across the tide provides a good example of the precision required. The target species – brill, turbot and blonde ray – will be found in the lee of the top of the bank, so the fishfinder must be used to identify the exact point and depth, enabling your lines can be trotted downtide and over the bank to the feeding fish.

ANGLING ON THE DRIFT

Sea anglers often choose to drift if they are aiming to catch species that are themselves on the move. Shoaling fish like cod can prove elusive from an anchored boat. On the drift, the boat moves with the tide and can cover a vast area. Because of this the angler is more likely to intercept mobile or isolated shoals of fish.

When used on the drift, the fishfinder takes on a slightly different role. The slow movement of the boat provides an ideal opportunity for tuning the fishfinder for optimum fish detection, and you should increase the chart speed and sensitivity settings accordingly.

Similarly you should activate the greyline facility to provide a detailed picture of the type of sea bed the boat is drifting over. A fishfinder can easily differentiate between rock, sand, and soft mud.

During the course of a long drift you may, for example, pass from clean sand to an isolated rock outcrop. This feature is very likely to attract a variety of fish. The fishfinder will not only detect those fish, but will also show the rock which returns a stronger signal. Rocky bottoms are usually uneven or jagged and will be displayed as such, with a sharp sea bed trace and a wider greyline.

A successful drift can be duplicated by moving back uptide of the 'hot spot' to cover the productive ground again. Drift duplication is even easier with the aid of a GPS plotter. This enables you to view the boat's track while at the same time watching the picture on the fishfinder.

WRECK FISHING

Wrecking has become one of the most popular activities engaged in by boat anglers. The quantity and quality of fish such as cod, pollack, and conger encountered around deepwater wrecks provides a natural attraction, and there is an element of discovery and drama associated with the whole business.

You can either anchor or drift over a wreck, but you are most likely to achieve success if you have a precise knowledge of the wreck's layout and orientation.

A series of slow passes over the wreck, both parallel to and across the tide, can indicate how the wreck is lying in relation to the tide, the maximum height of the wreck above the sea bed, other wreckage in the area, and obviously where the shoals of fish are hiding.

You may see pollack shoals off the bottom above the wreck. The usual way to catch pollack is by drifting, using live or artificial sandeels (redgills). You should obviously concentrate your efforts on the zone indicated by the fishfinder as containing the pollack.

Cod are often found close to the sea bed, in the lee and downtide of wrecks, and can be caught by drifting using pirks and baited feathers. I well remember finding a shoal between 400 and 600 metres downtide of a wreck. We had retrieved our lines from a previous drift ready for another when fish were detected by the fishfinder. Four of us proceeded to boat around 60 cod averaging 12 lb apiece – and all a long way from the wreck. Who says fishfinders don't catch fish!

The types of echo sounders we have described are not only used by anglers and divers for recreational purposes. These machines are also used extensively by organisations like construction companies working in marine environments, public service organisations such as the National Rivers Authority, and the scientific community, particularly marine biologists, for underwater research work. Inshore commercial fishermen and charter skippers also use them, although the larger commercial boats opt for more specialised, powerful sounders, and of course scanning sonar which requires large underwater housings to hold the retractable transducers.

In the UK, the fisheries department of the National Rivers Authority have used fishfinders to combat illegal netting, particularly for salmon, both in estuaries and in restricted areas at sea. Not only are the sounders used to locate the nets, but paper traces have been used as court evidence in cases where the headropes were not the required distance underwater.

Many police diving sections use echo sounders, particularly in the US where the search and rescue units find they save both time and manpower in the search for victims of drowning.

LOCH NESS AND MORAR PROJECT

Since the late 1970s a team of researchers has been studying in detail the biology of Britain's two deepest freshwater lakes – Loch Ness with a maximum depth of 230 metres and Loch Morar at 310 metres – and echo sounders have proved to be a particularly valuable research tool on the project.

Loch Ness is about 22 miles long and a mile wide, having virtually parallel sides except for the area of Urquhart Bay on its northern shore. Extending over a section of the geological fault line know as the Great Glen in the northern half of Scotland, it holds the greatest volume of

BELOW **A police diving team at Wastwater in the English Lake District, about to start a search for a drowned diver using a Lowrance X16.**

PLANNING A SEARCH

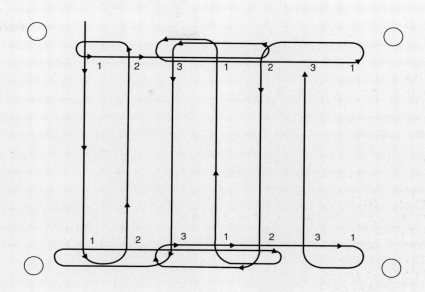

Searching a pond or lake by touch for a victim of drowning can be a time-consuming exercise for divers. Using a sounder can speed up the process dramatically, but only if you use a systematic search pattern.

The diagram above shows the best procedure for an area of roughly 50 by 100 metres. The circles at the four corners represent large marker buoys, while the numbers indicate small marker buoys that can be retrieved at the end of each lap.

Any suspect object can be quickly marked and checked from several angles as shown below. When the object first shows on the graph, drop a buoy immediately behind the boat. Then approach this buoy from 180 degrees and drop another as soon as the object is recorded. Repeat the process from 90-degree angles until the object is marked from four directions. The object should be lying at the exact centre of the four floats.

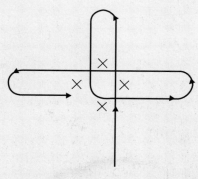

fresh water in the British Isles – more than all the water in the lakes and reservoirs of England and Wales combined. Soundings show very steeply sloping sides leading down to an almost flat, featureless bottom.

For most people the loch's main claim to fame is the Loch Ness Monster. Over the last 60 years, there have been several sightings of mysterious creatures in and around the loch, although firm evidence has been hard to come by in spite of many well-organised surveillance operations. The loch does however contain much of verifiable scientific interest.

Paper recording echo sounders, including Eagle Mach 1 and Mach 2 units, have been installed on rafts moored in the centre of the loch to monitor lateral and horizontal movements of fish and plankton in relation to the position of the thermocline. They are also used to observe the descent of the grabs used to obtain samples of the loch bed, so that they can be slowed just before reaching the bed to minimise the effect of impact.

The thermocline, normally an unwanted extra, has also been closely examined by the sounders, and particularly striking pictures of an underwater temperature surge wave were recorded in October 1985. This occurred after a period of strong south-westerly winds which had pushed the warmer surface water to the northern end of the loch. When this wind subsided, the warmer water slid back along the length of the loch preceded by the wave shown in the trace below.

Operation Deepscan

The Operation Deepscan survey of Loch Ness in 1987 had three objectives: to look for strong contacts in deep water – that is below 50 metres, which is about the fish limit – to chart objects of interest on the loch bed for later investigation, and to continue the general scientific programme of fish and thermocline observation.

The operation involved 19 boats in line abreast, each fitted with a Lowrance X16 echo sounder, making two complete passes along the length of the loch – in effect, sweeping it with an ultrasonic curtain.

Two major problems had to be overcome. First, the steeply shelving loch sides threatened to reflect side lobe echoes, producing false returns near the shores of the loch that would appear as ghost bottoms on the traces. Second, the close proximity of the boats (only 45 metres apart) was likely to cause interference between the sounders, and this would appear as grainy black marks on the trace. All this would severely compromise any interesting deep water returns.

BELOW **The thermocline produced by the wave of warm water moving down Loch Ness in October 1985 (Eagle Mach 2).**

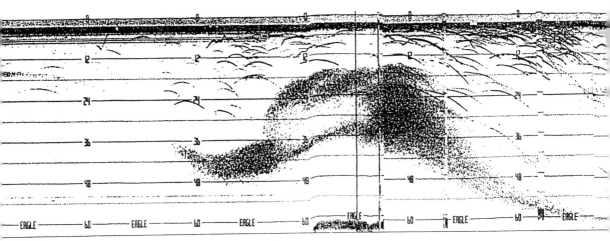

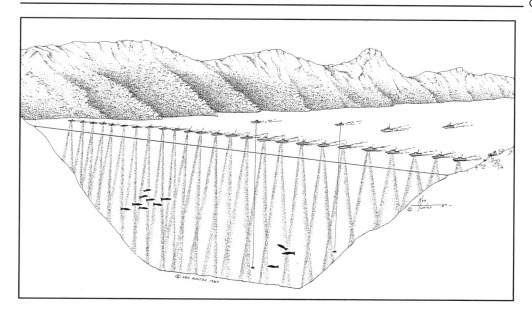

Although the original plan involved the line of boats stretching right across the loch, virtually from shore to shore, it became apparent that the only way to prevent the false echoes from the steeply sloping loch sides was to reduce the width of the sweep so that the line stopped short of the loch margins.

The interference between sounders was kept to a minimum because of the versatility of the X16. It had been decided to use them mainly in their low-frequency 50 kHz mode to achieve the best depth penetration using 30-degree beam transducers. The beamwidth was selected to give minimum overlap of the beams on the loch bed. The first stage in reducing the potential for interference was to reset every fourth sounder in the line to the high 192 kHz mode; in fresh water, using an eight-degree beam, the X16 on this setting showed a good bottom signal, even at a depth of 230 metres. Three different pulse lengths were used on the remaining 50 kHz units, so that the same combination of frequency and pulse length was limited to every fourth boat in the line. In this way, and by judicious use of the discrimination control, the potential for mutual interference was kept to a minimum.

Naturally the results that created most public interest were the deep water contacts, of which three were made on the southbound sweep. A copy of the largest of these contacts is shown below. It was actually picked up by one of the back-up craft, and shows a large object at a depth of about 190 metres. It was not spotted by the main fleet during either of the two sweeps – proof perhaps of its animate nature!

BELOW **The deep water contact.**

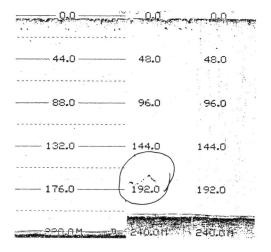

16 TROUBLESHOOTING ·······················

We have already looked at the care and maintenance of paper recorders in Chapter 7. Liquid crystal and video sounders have no moving parts, and for this reason should require little in the way of maintenance apart from keeping the screen clean, and keeping the plug and socket connections free from dirt and grit.

Any electronic faults in these units have to be repaired either by the manufacturer or a main distributor employing trained service engineers. Owners, however well qualified, are not encouraged to open up the sets, and doing so will almost certainly invalidate any guarantee. Waterproof models in particular need refilling with nitrogen from a special gas filling rig after service. Furthermore, the cases of some of the very latest sets are ultrasonically welded to produce a total seal, and therefore cannot be opened up; which means that faulty units have to be repaired on a service exchange basis.

Check that your retailer is part of the national authorised dealer network. If not, you could suffer a long delay if you need to have a set repaired under warranty. Unauthorised outlets also tend to lose interest once the statutory guarantee period has passed.

If your set appears to be faulty it is well worth checking a few possible reasons for your problem before sending the unit back to a service centre.

Won't turn on
1 Check the power lead at the battery end for proper polarity (red positive, black negative) and for corrosion.
2 Is the battery connected and master switch on?
3 Check the fuse and fuse connections.
4 Check power connector plug and display socket for corrosion or missing pins.

Rainbow or burnt spot on display
Remove sunglasses!

Weak bottom or no fish
1 Increase the sensitivity.
2 Check the transducer installation, particularly if in-hull. Has it broken away from its epoxy base?
3 Check the transducer for damage.
4 Check the transducer cable for cracks and breaks.

Erratic or false digital readings
1 Check transducer angle and installation
2 Use a short pulse length, if available.
3 Use low to medium surface clutter control (SCC).
4 Use discrimination control, if available.

Black or grainy screen at low speed
1 Sensitivity too high.
2 Check transducer installation.
3 Increase the surface clutter control (SCC).
4 Increase discrimination or fine echo if available.

Unit locks up or operates erratically
This could be due to electrical noise.
1 Try running the power lead direct to the battery.
2 Ensure the power lead is well away from sources of electrical noise such as ignition wires, alternators and electric bilge pumps.
3 Switch off the set and re-start it.

Sounders can be run and tested out of water without damaging them. Bear in mind, though, that there is severe attenuation of the signal when the transducer is shooting through air, even when the transducer is aimed directly at a hard object, so it will not register anything on the display more than a few feet away. Furthermore, since the speed of sound is about five times slower in air than in water, anything the transducer is aimed at will register on the display about at about five times the distance.

GLOSSARY ···

Adscope (also called A-scope) *see* fishlupe.

Advanced Signal Processing (ASP) Constant evaluation of water conditions, boatspeed and interference sources to adjust settings for best picture possible.

Bottom Lock The sea bed is displayed as a straight line, so that the exact height of fish above the sea bed can be determined.

Bottom Track The ability to follow and not lose the contours of the sea bed while in zoom mode.

Cavitation Air bubbles created by the rotation of a propeller.

Chart speed The speed that the chart paper moves under the stylus on a paper recording sounder, or the speed that the image moves across the screen of a LCG or video sounder (also called scrolling speed).

Cone angle The angle of the path followed by the transmitted ultrasonic pulse, normally about 20 degrees.

Cursor A movable line that can be positioned over a target to give its actual depth.

CRT Cathode Ray Tube, as used in video sounders.

Definition The ability to display detail on the screen, often described as the number of pixels in the vertical dimension.

Discrimination As a control, the facility that removes unwanted noise without reducing sensitivity by comparing the echoes on the returning pulse with these on the preceding pulse (also known as Clean Echo).

Fastrak *see* fishlupe.

Fish alarm An alarm that activates when the sounder detects objects above a preprogrammed size.

Fish ID The processing of the echoes to show them as fish shapes on the screen. The size of the shape is often relative to the strength of the echo.

Fishlupe The expansion of each received pulse to fill a large part or all of the screen (also called Adscope, A-scope and Fastrak).

GRP Glass reinforced plastic, i.e. fibreglass.

Gain See sensitivity.

Gimbal bracket The display mounting bracket.

Greyline A method of processing the picture so that the bottom is displayed as a thin black ribbon over a greyish band to determine bottom hardness and make identification of wrecks and bottom-feeding fish easier (also called white line).

kHz Kilohertz, the operating frequency in cycles per second.

In-hull See shoot-through-hull.

LCD Liquid crystal display.

LCG Liquid crystal graph.

Noise Any unwanted signal showing as interference in the form of random dots or lines on the display.

Pixel The small dots or squares that make up the liquid crystal display. Stands for picture element.

Pixel density The number of pixels per square inch of display. The greater the number, the higher the resolution of the display. The number of pixels vertically is far more important than the number horizontally.

Power output The energy transmitted by the transducer, measured in watts.

Preset This enables sets with memory back up to be reset to their original factory settings.

Pulse length Determined by the length of time that the echo sounder transmits its signal.

Range The height of the column of water chosen for display on the screen.

Resolution (1) The ability of the machine to separate individual echoes or targets from each other or from the bottom. (2) Can also refer to the pixel density of the screen.

Secondary echo A mirror-image bottom

echo, appearing at double the depth. In shallow water, a third and sometimes fourth bottom can be seen.

Second function key Found on some of the earlier LCGs, this converts some of the buttons on the keypad to operate another function.

Sensitivity The ability to adjust the target size displayed on the screen (also called gain).

Scroll speed *see* chart speed.

Shoot-through-hull A transducer that can be bonded onto the inside of the hull (also called in-hull). Can only be used on GRP hulls.

Side lobe A small part of the ultrasonic pulse that is transmitted sideways instead of downwards.

Spike A pulse of high voltage.

Stylus The piece of wire that marks the paper on a paper sounder.

Suppression A control found on some paper graphs to eliminate noise.

Surface Clutter The noise caused by air bubbles and plankton in the top few feet of water.

Surface Clutter Control A control to reduce the effect of surface clutter by adjusting the sensitivity in that area of the display. Also called Sensitivity Time Control (STC) and Time Variable Gain (TVG).

Targets Any echoes or marks above the bottom.

Thermocline The boundary between water of different temperatures.

Through-hull A transducer that is mounted through a hole in the hull.

Transducer The element that converts electrical energy into an ultrasonic pulse that it then transmits into the water; it then converts the returning pulse back into electrical energy which is sent to the display.

Transom mount A popular method of mounting the transducer on the transom of the boat.

Triducer A transducer with a paddle wheel for a speed and distance log, plus a temperature sensor.

Upper/lower limit A feature enabling a specific range to be shown on the screen, entered by a calculator-type keypad.

Video graph A television-type display using a cathode ray tube.

Window A specific depth range, i.e. if the sounder showed a range of between 40 and 60 feet when used in the zoom mode, it would display a 20-foot window.

Windows Ability to split the screen into a number of rectangles to display different pieces of information at the same time.

Zone alarm An alarm that sounds when an echo or the bottom picture enters a pre-set area of the screen.

Zoom The ability to reduce the range displayed on the screen to increase the size of the targets.

GPS GLOSSARY

Anywhere fix The ability of a receiver to get a fix without the need to input time and position information, also known as Cold Start.

Almanac Data about future satellite positions sent down by satellite and stored by the receiver.

Azimuth The compass bearing expressed in degrees.

C/A Code The standard Coarse Acquisition code information transmitted by GPS satellites.

Cold start *see* Anywhere fix.

Course Deviation Indicator (CDI) Visual display of cross-track error.

Channel Each channel of a GPS receiver has the circuitry necessary to tune the signal from a single GPS satellite.

Course Over Ground (COG) The actual course of the boat, including the leeway caused by any tide.

Cross-track Error (XTE) The distance away from track when navigating to a waypoint.

Differential positioning The measurement of the same signals by two receivers, one of which is at a known position, to give a very precise fix.

Dilution Of Precision (DOP) The error in position caused by the angles between the receiver and satellites.

Elevation The height of the satellite expressed in degrees above the horizon.

Ephemeris The predictions of current satellite positions that are transmitted to the user in a data message.

Fix The position on a chart shown by the navigator.

Horizontal Dilution Of Precision (HDOP) *see* dilution of precision.

Multiplex receiver A single-channel receiver which rapidly samples a number of satellite signals.

Multi-channel receiver A GPS receiver that can track several satellites at the same time.

P-code The precise code only available for military use.

Pseudo-random code The signal transmitted by the satellites to the receivers, with an almost random appearance.

Pseudo-range The distance initially calculated to the satellite before delays and errors have been included.

Route A sequence of waypoints programmed into the receiver.

Selective availability The deliberate degrading of the signal by the US government to protect military sites.

Signal to Noise Ratio (SNR) Indicates how good the satellite signal is compared to the noise or interference level.

Speed Over the Ground (SOG) The actual speed of the boat relative to the sea bed.

Time Dilution Of Precision (TDOP) *see* dilution of precision.

Track The shortest distance between your present position and your waypoint, i.e. a straight line.

Universal Coordinated Time The standard time used by GPS systems (for all practical purposes Greenwich Mean Time).

Vertical Dilution Of Precision (VDOP) *see* dilution of precision.

Waypoint Any chosen position entered into the receiver as a destination.

Also published by Fernhurst Books

Beaufort Scale Cookbook *by June Raper*

Boat Engines *by Dick Hewitt*

Celestial Navigation *by Tom Cunliffe*

Coastal & Offshore Navigation *by Tom Cunliffe*

Electronics Afloat *by Tim Bartlett*

First Aid Afloat *by Dr Robert Haworth*

Heavy Weather Cruising *by Tom Cunliffe*

Inshore Navigation *by Tom Cunliffe*

Knots and Splices *by Jeff Toghill*

Log Book for Cruising under Power *by Tom Willis & Tim Bartlett*

Log Book for Cruising under Sail *by John Mellor*

Marine SSB Operation *by Michael Gale*

Marine VHF Operation *by Michael Gale*

Motor Boating *by Alex McMullen*

Navigation at Speed *by Tim Bartlett*

Powerboating *by Peter White*

Radar *by Tim Bartlett*

Rules of the Road *by John Mellor*

Simple Electronic Navigation *by Mik Chinery*

Tides and Currents *by David Arnold*

Weather at Sea *by David Houghton*

Fernhurst Books are available from all good bookshops and chandleries. In case of difficulty, or if you would like a copy of our full cataloque, please send your name and address to:

Fernhurst Books, 33 Grand Parade, Brighton, East Sussex BN2 2QA, UK